THE GODS OF OLYMPIA STADIUM

LEGENDS OF THE DETROIT RED WINGS

BY

RICHARD KINCAIDE

WWW.SPORTSPUBLISHINGLLC.COM

Director of production
SUSAN. M. MOYER

Developmental editor
GABE A. ROSEN

Book design, senior project manager
JENNIFER L. POLSON

Dust jacket design
KENNETH J. O'BRIEN

Photo imaging
KENNETH J. O'BRIEN AND CHRISTINE MOHRBACHER

Copy editors
CYNTHIA L. McNEW AND HOLLY BIRCH

ISBN 1-58261-601-9

Printed in the United States.

This book is dedicated to the men who herein tell their stories. They gave me gold and told me to make something nice out of it.

And to Bill Jamieson, whose witness and wisdom touch all who know him.

CONTENTS

Courtesy of Robert L. Wimmer

FOREWORD

The day I interviewed Red Kelly for this book, more than 42 years had passed since that night in February of 1960 when—following a 3-1 loss to the New York Rangers at Detroit's Olympia Stadium—Jack Adams, the general manager of the Detroit Red Wings, called Kelly to his office to inform his eight-time All-Star defenseman that he had been traded to New York.

This book will tell you what Red had to say about this surprising development. That is all it can do. It cannot show you the fists he clenched or the anger that overtook over his face. You cannot hear his voice quake. The words are all there, but you can't see, as I did, that his reaction was deeply visceral—42 years removed from the injustice!

Nor can this book show you the one thing that made the deepest impression on me during dozens of interviews: The look on Andra Kelly's face when her husband was discussing how they would, from time to time, tape over fractured bones so Red wouldn't have to take a night off. Every husband knows "The Look:" The face of amazement staring at us, dumbfounded and angry, knowing we're doing something that's really too foolish for words; something the result of

which is likely a serious injury ("What did you expect, you big dummy?"). And with it, the face of utter contempt reserved for anyone responsible for putting us in such a position to begin with. In Red Kelly's case, that would be his boss, Jack Adams.

Fifty years have gone by since she first met him, and Andra Kelly still is shaking her head about Jack Adams. And she is not alone.

Jack Adams played in the National Hockey League starting in 1917—the first year there was a National Hockey League. He coached the Detroit Red Wings for 20 years, starting in 1927. He was the general manager for 36. He ran the show. He was dead, at 72, only six years after he was fired by Red Wings Owner Bruce Norris after the 1962 season.

This book is about the Detroit Red Wings of the 1940s, '50s, and '60s. It is, therefore, a book about Jack Adams.

Red Kelly never swears. He played for 20 years in a league where somebody like Ted Lindsay would "put that stick right in your mouth"—and, still, he never, ever, swears. It may have helped that

Lindsay and Kelly were on-ice opponents in only four of those seasons, but still….

Red was talking about the trade by Adams of Detroit goaltender Glenn Hall to Chicago and wanted to give me an exact quote. But to do so would involve using a very bad word, indeed. So he leaned forward, looked around to make sure Andra wasn't nearby, and whispered the first letter of the word in question to me. His concern was that I, as a reporter, would get from him that which I needed the most—accuracy—and he was darn near ready to violate a personal principle to get it done.

They were all like that.

There are two features I think are peculiar to this book and, as such, are of interest to the reader. The first is directed particularly at younger readers.

And it is this: If you have a mind to, you can go out and write a book like this yourself.

Fifty-two years went by before it occurred to me that it might be interesting to talk to some of the guys, some of the Detroit Red Wings, who won the Stanley Cup in 1950. They were members of a club that went on to win four Cup championships in six seasons.

Let 52 years go by from, say, 1996 when the current crop of Red Wings began their run of Stanley Cup glory. The year then would be 2048. Steve Yzerman would be 83…   Sergei Fedorov, 79…Darren McCarty, 76….

What might their memories be then, somewhere down the trail?

What might they think of the contemporary game—hockey as it is being played not at the beginning of the 21st century, but in the middle of the 21st century?

Those memories and observations are what I sought from the players who tell you their stories in this book.

Should you undertake the effort, if your experience in 2048 is anything like mine in 2003, I can tell you one thing with absolute certainty: In writing your book, you will meet amazing gentlemen. You will meet men who will inspire you. And you will learn, as I did, why they were heroes to their generation.

The other feature of note regarding this book is aimed at the reader who may be pressed for time. If you want to understand this book in its totality, all you have to do is read the first sentence of the first chapter.

Richard Kincaide
April, 2003

THE GODS OF OLYMPIA STADIUM

LEGENDS OF THE DETROIT RED WINGS

#4

BILL GADSBY

NATIONAL HOCKEY LEAGUE 1946-1966
CHICAGO BLACKHAWKS 1946-52
NEW YORK RANGERS 1952-60
DETROIT RED WINGS 1960-66
DETROIT RED WINGS HEAD COACH 1968-1969
HOCKEY HALL OF FAME 1971

I'LL TELL YOU ONE THING: It was a great life, playing in the NHL. I know. I was a defenseman in the National Hockey League for 20 years. I played for three teams—half the clubs that were in the league then. If you played for half the teams that are in the league today, you'd have to play for *15* teams! I started with the Chicago Blackhawks, got traded to the New York Rangers, and later to the Detroit Red Wings.

You couldn't beat the hours.

Sure, the money wasn't like it is today, but it was good. It was better than good—way better. I signed my first contract with the Chicago Blackhawks in 1946 when I was 18 years old.

I got $8,500 for the season, and I got a $3,500 signing bonus. Big money? It was like getting $3 million!

Just as soon as my rookie year was over, I drove up to the GM factory in Oshawa and picked up my first car—a brand-new 1947 Chevy. One thousand nine hundred and fifty bucks for a brand new Chevrolet; how about that?

I drove it straight from the factory in Oshawa all the way home to Edmonton. What a time I had! And when I come home to Edmonton with that one, with that brand-new automobile, man, I was a big wheel. I was the only one who had wheels. All my buddies at home, they didn't have cars. That was really something.

I bought all the beer all summer. They might have been making two or three thousand dollars, my buddies. I was making $8,500. And I was doing it in seven months. That's all we played, at the most. What I time I had!

OPPOSITE: **Bill Gadsby.**
(Photo courtesy of Robert L. Wimmer)

A loaf of bread was 10 cents in those days. A pound of hamburger was two bits, 25 cents. So everything's relative, you know? I had plenty of cash.

We got the shaft in certain ways, though. We weren't getting the money we should have, probably. I spent eight years in Chicago and seven in New York, and I argued over money the whole time. Fifteen years. But I never had to argue here in Detroit. Jack Adams was the general manager, and then Sid Abel after him, and they were very good to me.

But those first 15 years!

In Chicago I make the second All-Star Team in 1952. I'm on my way to Jasper Park Lodge up in the Rocky Mountains in Alberta for a little family vacation before training camp. The day we leave, I check the mail and there's my contract.

We're in the car, so I say to Edna, my wife, "Open it up. I've got to be getting a raise, making the All-Star Team last year."

Edna opens it up and shows it to me. I can't believe it. It's the same contract. The same damn thing as the year before! And I'm thinking, "That's not right. You make the All-Star Team, first team or second, you've got to get a raise. You're top four in the league!"

So I get to Jasper and I'm pissed off. I write Chicago Blackhawks a letter on Jasper Lodge Stationery and send the contract back. Told them I wanted a three- or four-thousand-dollar raise.

We spend a week up there, and when I get back home to Edmonton, I get this letter from Mr. Bill Tobin, general manager and part owner of the Chicago Blackhawks.

We've still got that letter. It starts out:

Dear Mr. Gadsby:

You are either staying up late with your new baby or the altitude in the Canadian Rockies has gone to your head for you to be asking for this type of a raise.

My wife said, "We've got to keep that." And we did. It's the first thing in our scrapbook, in fact. We've had more fun with that letter over the course of the last 40 years or so.

"The baby must be keeping you up."

"The altitude's gone to your head."

Can you imagine them sending a player a letter like that *now*?

So I held out. I missed a week of training camp. First time in my life, and the only time in my life, I was late to camp. But I'd been in the league six or seven years, and making the All-Star Team, I said, "What the hell, I've got to get *something*."

Those days, though, you knew damn well there were eight or 10 guys down in the farm system who weren't too shabby, so that's always in the back of your mind.

A few years ago in Canada, they made that movie about Teddy Lindsay trying to start an NHL Players' Association in 1957 that they called *Net Worth*. It made us players look like we really were getting the shaft, like we were all struggling to get by.

Let me tell you something: Life in the NHL wasn't *anything* like *Net Worth* made it out to be. That movie had a lot of BS in it, a lot. I told Teddy Lindsay, "I think you wrote it, produced it, and directed it."

I was player representative for New York Rangers in the '50s—and, remember, there were only six teams. So there were only six of us player reps. I was one of them, but when I watched the movie, I didn't even know which one I was supposed to be.

There was a lot of stuff in *Net Worth* that wasn't true. For example, they showed a veteran Detroit player who'd been cut by Jack Adams. The guy winds up living in his car, and he ends up dying in his car when it catches fire one night while he's asleep inside.

I phoned Gordie Howe the day after it was on and asked him, "Who was the guy in the Olympia Stadium parking lot, the player who died in a fire while he was living in his car?"

He said, "What the hell are you talking about?"

I said, "Well, I was playing for the Rangers, so I know I wasn't here in Detroit then, but you were. And in that *Net Worth* story there's a guy who was having some financial problems who was playing for the Red Wings, and they found him dead in his car."

Gordie said, "That's bull. I never heard anything about that."

So I knew right then that it wasn't true.

Gordie Howe. He could do everything. God, he could shoot the puck. Gordie had a slapshot, but it was only eight inches long. His stick would come back just about like that, but he would kind of whip it. He could get that puck away so quick. That's why he's got a lot of goals, of course.

He was big and strong, Gordie was. I played against him 15 years, I know. But I can tell you one thing about Howe: If you played it straight up with him, you had no problem. But if you give him the stick or the butt-end or the elbow in the mouth, or whatever you're going to do, you better look out, because he was going to get you. Might not be that night, might not be for another month or two, but he was going to get you.

He didn't mind the holding. He was so strong. Him and Rocket Richard were probably the two strongest guys I played against. They'd stick that arm out and ward you off, and there wasn't much you could do. Maybe put the hook on 'em. You know, you gotta put it on and take it off quick. Just a little bit of a hook, make him get off stride, or whatever. But you couldn't hook and hook and hook. Today the stickwork is terrible. They're up too high, and I think those helmets and masks and half-shields have a lot to do with it.

We had kind of an unwritten rule that the stick never came up over the waist. I see them today backchecking on guys with the stick around their neck, then pulling them back! Some nights it looks like they're chopping trees out there. The slashing is terrible. There's more stickwork today, a lot more.

You don't see as much center-ice hitting. That's what we did a lot of in my era. There's a lot of boarding going on now. The NHL really has to watch this checking from behind, the crosschecking into the boards. Somebody's going to break their neck, and it's going to be a tragedy on the NHL. Somebody's *got to*, the way they bang those guys into the boards.

We used to take 'em out, but it wasn't that vicious. That I remember.

All I did was try to hit guys in a fair way. More to get their attention, you know? Maybe take a little out of them. I never run at somebody and give 'em the stick and the like. I put the hip check on a lot of guys, a lot. That's the best way. Or straight up, if the guy's got his head down.

I hit Tim Horton that way in Toronto one night. Broke his jaw and broke his leg all in one body check. Right just this side of center ice; he had his head down. You know, I can honestly say I hardly felt the check. I knew I hit him good.

No penalty. Bill Chadwick was refereeing then; old Bill Chadwick. He was the senior referee in the league.

When Horton went down, I took a look at him, and the blood was coming out of the corner of his mouth and out his ear. And I got scared. "Gee," I thought, "he may be dead."

I was shook up that night. When I went off the ice, Connie Smythe, the owner of Toronto Maple Leafs, met me going down the hallway.

He said, "You son of a bitch. I'll have you suspended for that body check. I'll get you suspended for trying to injure one of my best players, you rotten bastard!"

I just turned around and told him to —— off. And I kept on walking. I felt bad as it was. Turns out it set Tim Horton back two years.

Two of his teammates, Billy Harris and Frank Mahovlich, told me Horton was far and away the strongest guy on the Toronto Maple Leafs. But I just caught him right. He had his head down, and my shoulder caught him right in the jaw. And I hardly felt it.

They had a program on a couple of years ago on *Hockey Night in Canada*, with Ron MacLean and Don Cherry, and they made a survey of all the old ushers and usherettes in Toronto Maple Leaf Gardens. They asked them what was the hardest body check they had ever seen, and that check of mine on Tim Horton was number one, by far. That's how hard I hit him. There's been a ton of them in Maple Leaf Gardens, too— body checks. I don't have to tell you that. And they say that was the hardest of them all.

Oh, I knew I hurt him. Like I said, I didn't feel very good about it. You don't want to maim a guy. I don't, anyway.

Now some guys, like John Mariucci, he'd like to hope the son of a bitch may be dead. That's the type he was. Ever hear of him? John Mariucci. He was on the Blackhawks when I broke into the NHL in November, 1946. Mariucci was from Minnesota, and he stuck out,

were taking turns hitting each other, just to see who was going to go down first.

And I'm saying to myself, *"Did I pick the right profession? Am I in the right place? Man, oh man. What have I gotten myself into?"*

It was a fight-filled game, and we ended up with a minute, minute and a half to go with three men on each side on the ice. I'm sitting on the

"And I'm saying to myself, 'Did I pick the right profession? Am I in the right place? Man, oh man. What have I gotten myself into?'"

—BILL GADSBY

believe me. He was an All-American at the University of Minnesota. He became the athletic director up there when he retired. They got a rink up there named after him. John Mariucci was the toughest guy I've ever seen play the game of hockey—the *meanest and the toughest*!

It was either my second or third game in Chicago, and him and Jack Stewart of Detroit got in a fight. They hit each other for two to three minutes on the ice. I knew Stewart was a tough guy, and I knew Mariucci was a mean, tough bastard from playing with him.

In those days, they only had one penalty box, and in they go together. Both of them are cut up. Their noses, chins, and mouths are all bloody and bleeding. They started up again. And they beat the —— out of each other. They

bench, and Max and Doug Bentley come over to the bench. Max led the league in scoring that season, and Doug was in the top 10, so you knew they were going to be out there, those two guys.

Johnny Gottselig is the coach. He played for something like 16 years for Chicago—from 1928 all the way through the war, before they made him the coach. Johnny Gottselig was born in Russia, did you know? I've wondered if that might not make Johnny Gottselig the first Russian in the NHL.

So Gottselig asks the Bentleys, "Who do you want out there with you?"

And both of them said at the same time, "Give us the kid." They meant me.

So I went out, and at 19:59, I scored the winning goal against the Detroit Red Wings off Harry Lumley. That's still one of my all-time highlights.

"Apple Cheeks" Harry Lumley broke into the NHL when he was only 17. A few years later, in the early '50s, Lum and I played together in Chicago. I wasn't married then, and we had an apartment in Chicago. I roomed with him on the road, too. Lum is gone now. Good guy. Good goalie, too.

But that John Mariucci! Mariucci took care of the Bentley brothers and Bill Mosienko, our best players in Chicago. Guys would hit the Bentleys with a bad check, a stick check, or into the boards; Mariucci would go after them just like it had been his own son. And he would beat the piss out of them. He'd beat them up!

Big Doug McCaig, who played here in Detroit—he was about 6'4" probably weighed 220—he hit Max Bentley one night at center ice with a bad check. I mean, really bad. Mariucci was in our corner and he started skating toward McCaig, picking up speed as he went. McCaig was just getting up off the ice. Mariucci had his fist closed for the whole way, about 60 feet. He hit McCaig right here in the jaw and lifted him right up off of the ice.

Twenty years later, our trainer here in Detroit, Lefty Wilson, told me Doug McCaig didn't know where he was for *three days*. They came back by train, and he didn't know what hit him, where he was, or anything. Knocked him cold turkey, Lefty told me. And McCaig was a big, big man.

Mariucci used to get charley horses. He'd be all bruised up. He'd get a bottle of that Capsoline they had. It's a liniment. It's hotter than a son of a bitch. I'd put it on sometimes, and I had to go get a wet towel and rub it off, it's so damn hot. He would take a shower in it! He'd slather it on both legs. And he'd play. He'd just hobble out of the dressing room and play. I've never seen a guy like that.

The referees had their hands full. When I first came into the league, it was Bill Chadwick, Red Story or King Clancy refereeing.

I never did like those bastards, anyway—the officials, that is. I had a lot of trouble with them. But in those days—it's not like it is today—we could talk to them.

Red Story used to say, "Bill, if you're going to talk to me, just *don't look* at me. If you're going to say something, *you look away* and you say, 'You blind so and so! How come you missed that?' Or, 'That was a lousy penalty!' Don't come over and get right in my face, because you're bleeping going to go right away if you do!"

And that meant a misconduct penalty. And that meant 25 bucks out of your pocket. That's what a misconduct cost you—a lot of money.

But Story was funny. You'd hook a guy, or do something that wasn't right, and you'd hear him yell, "I saw it! Don't think I didn't see it! But don't do it again! One more of those, you're going!" Oh, yeah.

We had a pretty good rapport with most referees. Frank Udvari and I never did get along too good. I didn't like him. Or Art Skov, for that matter.

I'd yell, "Skov! You're a homer, you bastard!"

We'd come in here to play Detroit, and we all knew he lived in Windsor, and his brother Glen had played for Detroit. Sure, we thought Skov was a homer. At the time we did.

I'll tell you about a guy who gave the referees fits. Howie Young. Howie Young was a character, a big-time character. I roomed with him. His nickname was "Wild Thing." He was bad news.

Did Huey miss many curfews? He never *made* one. I've never seen a guy like him, never. Drinking and then he got into that other funny stuff. He wasn't much of a hockey player, but he was colorful.

Our coach in Detroit, Sid Abel, put Young on Bobby Hull in the playoffs. He did *a hell of a job.* Young's body was nicked from Hull spearing him. "Look at this!" he'd say. There were welts all over his body. I said, "Well, you're doing a good job. That won't hurt you. Don't worry about that. Just keep doing it." And he did. It drove Hull nuts. He'd like to kill him.

Young was nuts on the ice. I've seen him jumping on Bobby Hull's back. Backchecking Hull, and he jumped right on his back. Crazy!

Young could pester Hull because he could skate. He was a real good skater, in fact, but I think he was half jazzed-up all the time.

I'm sitting there one day before practice, and they had these pigeon holes where they'd put our checks and mail in the dressing room. Howie's yelling, coming back from when he got his check, and he sits down in front of me.

He says, "Gee, Bill. How do they expect me to live on this son of a bitch? *Look at this check!*"

"I don't want to look at your check," I said. Because in those days, nobody knew what everybody else was making. Today they *all* do, which is all right. But we never did. I didn't know what Gordie was making, or Alex Delvecchio, or Marcel Pronovost. I didn't care, either.

Howie says, "Damn it. You've got to look at this!"

So I did. The check was for *eight dollars and fifty cents*! On the other side of the check it said, "NHL Fine: $300; Club Fine: $250." All the way down. There must have been five items. "Missing Practice" and things like that. Gee, he'd miss practices, I don't know how many times. Or come late. Oh, it was bad. He got away with it for a long time. Finally, he didn't get away with it.

Sid would call me at home and say, "That bar on West Chicago Boulevard where you guys go? I just got a call from the barmaid. They want him out of there. Bill, go get him, will you?"

It's midnight. I go over, and only two or three people are in the place. I don't see him. I ask the barmaid if she called about Howie Young.

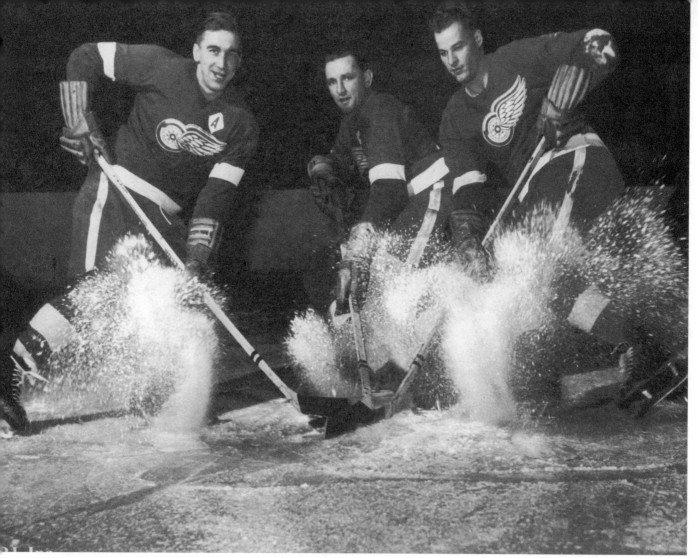

Ted Lindsay, Sid Abel and Gordie Howe. (Photo courtesy of Robert L. Wimmer)

She said, "Yes, but I don't know where the crazy bastard is. Maybe he's left."

I started walking out, and I see him in the little cubbyhole with the pay phone. He's sitting on the stool. And you talk about drunk. He rolled his own cigarettes, and he's got tobacco all over the front of his shirt and a rolling paper sticking out of his mouth. He's a mess.

He looks up at me and says, "What the hell are you doing here?"

He recognized me, at least. I didn't really know if he did or not, sometimes.

I told him to give me his keys, and we argued for 20 minutes. He wouldn't give me his keys until I said, "Okay, you SOB. You get in that car and I'm following you home."

He must have gone through 10 red lights. Now, I'm behind him, and I'm really looking to see if anything's coming. Couple of times, I had to slow down, and the other guy is blowing his horn because he went through. I don't know how he got home.

He does, though. Once he's there, he's trying to go up the steps on all fours. He passed out right there on the steps. He didn't even make it to the porch. Howie didn't play much that night. Two or three shifts maybe. Sid knew. You could really tell.

It happened all the time, too; all the time.

We're in Chicago. In the *playoffs*, mind you. Six or seven of us go out for dinner. Nice restaurant. Howie is there with us. I get back to the room; we had an 11:30 curfew. I'm rooming with Young. Sid calls the room, "Bill, is he in yet?"

I told him no.

Wait a half an hour, and Sid calls back. Howie is still not back. Sid says, "Wherever you guys had dinner, I want you to go there and see if the son of a bitch is still there!"

This is a quarter to one in the morning, now. So I get dressed and go down. It's only a couple of blocks down LaSalle Street.

I walk in and there's a guy—it's Howie, naturally—standing on the top of the bar with a pillow inside his shirt. I don't know where he got this pillow from, the washroom or something. He's got his shirt turned around, a white shirt, and he's got no teeth; he took his teeth out.

He's giving an impression of *The Hunchback of Notre Dame*. You should have seen him. He looked like *The Hunchback of Notre Dame*, he really did.

And he's stoned. And the crowd's clapping. They're sitting at the bar *cheering*, and he's walk-

ing, knocking bottles down. So I went down to the end of the bar and waited for him to come. It took him five or six minutes before he walked down to the end of the bar.

I said, "Huey, get that son of a bitching shirt the right way and get your ass and come on, let's go." And he came.

He didn't play very much that night, either. Sid was very disciplined in that way. He had to be, because the guys all knew.

Howie Young was the craziest son of gun I ever met. Crazy! But he straightened his life around. He got off the juice. He was clean for 20-some years. He lived in Gallup, New Mexico. He was teaching the Indians about alcoholism.

I talked to him 10 days before he died. He started crying, and his wife grabbed the phone. She said, "Billy, he just can't talk anymore." It was the alcohol that killed him way too young, I'm pretty sure, yes.

I was born and raised in Calgary. They didn't have any junior hockey in Calgary then. When I was 16, Edmonton approached me. The Edmonton Canadiens were one of the sponsored teams, and in those days if you played for them, you automatically became property of the Chicago Blackhawks. My dad was all for it. He said, as long as you get up there and finish your schooling and play hockey, we'll see what happens. So that's what I did. I went up there and played Junior. That was 1944. I was 16.

Two years later, in 1946, I turned pro.

I turned pro with guys like Bert Olmstead, who went on to play for years with Montreal, and Metro Prystai, who played for Detroit. They both played in the Saskatchewan League with the Moose Jaw Canucks.

We were all sent to the Kansas City Pla-Mors. It was in the USHL, the United States Hockey League. They had the Dallas Texans, Fort Worth Rangers, Houston Huskies, Tulsa Oilers, Minneapolis Millers and Omaha Knights in the league.

In my first pro game, my first game for the Pla-Mors, I got 26 stitches. A guy hit me over the head with his stick, a guy from Tulsa named Nick Knott. Me—a rookie and all—I took Mr. Knott into the corner and kind of rubbed him up a little bit. He got mad and turned around and hit me right over the head with his stick. Twenty-six stitches! My first pro game and the worst I ever got in 20 years pro.

That was the start of my stitch count. My wife's kept track of my stitches over the years, and it's over 650 stitches now. She kept track of 'em when I played in Chicago, New York and Detroit.

I never saw Nick Knott again. I only played 12 games in Kansas City, so I never got back to play him again—because I was going to get that bastard, some way.

I played 12 games for the Pla-Mors, and in the fall of '46, got called up by the parent club, by the Chicago Blackhawks. I got an assist my first game, which is good. I was surprised to get called up so soon. They had a couple of injuries.

I remember a lot of the players there in Chicago. We had the Bentleys—Doug and Max—Bill Mosienko, Johnny Mariucci. We didn't have very good clubs the years I was there. We finished last five of my first six years in the league, and we finished next to last the one year we *didn't* finish last. In 1953-54 we only won 12 games! That was the fewest in a season for over 20 years, until Washington won only eight in 1975. But I was just happy I was in the NHL.

In my second season, 1947, just a month in, we traded Max Bentley to Toronto. That was one of the biggest trades in hockey in the last 50-60 years! Max Bentley was the key in Chicago, our superstar. But those things happen. It was a five-for-two deal. We got Bud Poile and Bob Goldham, Gaye Stewart, Gus Bodnar and Ernie Dickens. Max went to Toronto. He led the Maple Leafs in scoring, and Toronto won the Stanley Cup. And, like I said, we didn't make the playoffs.

When I got called up, I got number four, which I wore for 20 years. I got a lower berth on the train because the low numbers got the lower berths. Sure, I was a rookie, but I had number four, and that's just how it worked. The defensemen all got low numbers, between number two and number six. That meant we all got the lower berths.

Maybe they thought we needed our sleep. See, we only carried five defensemen. And the fifth guy, he didn't see much action. I get a kick out of it today. They show defensemen playing 24-26 minutes a game. Hell, we used to play 30-35. If we didn't, we were mad.

What I tried to do in my career was get the play going. I don't think the game's changed that much. That's what Nicklas Lidstrom does, and that's what Chris Chelios does.

You make that first pass out of your own zone, and then you've done most of your job. Get it up! I learned that early in Chicago with a couple of the old-timers. Clint Smith—he played with the Rangers and he's in the Hall of Fame—and he'd say, "Bill, you've got to get the puck up. As soon as you get it, look. And if the guy's in position—the forward—you give it to him." And that stuck in my craw for years. Well, my whole career.

Look at Doug Harvey of Montreal. He was a great passer. I admired him in a way, but he beat me out of the Norris Trophy three times, three straight years! I'm just joking, I mean, it was always nice to be number two. And we made the All-Star Team together a few years. But he was good. He was good in his own end. He got the rush going.

Get it up, and you've done your job. And that's what they do today—they headman that puck. Oh, boy. They are so good.

The majority of the guys today shoot the puck a lot better than in my era. We had three or four on each club who could really shoot. To-day, they've got 15. They can *all* shoot the son of a bitch.

They're big. *They're so damn big.* Theo Fleury looks like a midget out there. But they can skate, for big guys. I admire them. They can really skate. Guys like Chris Pronger and Mike Modano and Eric Lindros. Those are big guys. They're very mobile. I'm very impressed with them.

I'm impressed with Steve Yzerman. I call him a combination of great reaction and very good coordination. He's something else, that Yzerman. I've met him four or five times. Nice fellow. Boy, he's got not one heart, but he's got two of them in his body, because the guy is unbelievable. He really is.

Yzerman comes and asks me if he could play in my era. I said, "Yeah, you'd probably be in the top seven or eight guys in the league."

Yzerman reminds me most probably of Henri Richard. Stevie's a little taller, but they both come to play every night.

Every night! And when Richard was on the ice, he was always in your hair. He was always there.

Another guy who really came to play every night was Ted Lindsay. He was a stick man. He would start a lot of stuff out on that ice that some-body else would finish. An agitator? Very much so; that's a good word. He'd start a lot of things on that ice. Guys would try to get at him, and they had to go through Gordie first, because Gordie would be on the ice at the same time.

But he was a good playmaker. Lindsay was tal-ented. He could score goals. Detroit got Teddy back in 1964-65. He'd been retired for four years, and he played really well. He came back and really helped us. He got 14 goals that year and Detroit finished first for the first time since 1957.

He was a mean sucker. He was one of the meanest guys who ever played in the NHL, Ted Lindsay. *He'd put that stick right in your mouth.* I saw him do some funny things when he came back in '64. Guys would take a run at him; they'd have to come through that lumber before they got to him, I'll tell you that.

Oh, he was in a lot of incidents in his career. Stick-swinging deals. He and Bill Ezinicki, a big guy from Toronto, had a few of them. He got in one with a couple of guys in Boston, too. But he took care of himself. He wasn't that big a guy; that's why he had to do it. A lot of guys would run at him, trying to nail him for something he did to them, but you had to come through the lumber first with Ted.

When we played against Chicago—Stan Mikita, I had his number. I hit him so hard so many times. And the son of a bitch would get up. He was a tough little bastard.

He had a habit of coming down and throwing the puck to his winger and then looking. And I'm coming from that other side, that blind side, and I hit him so hard some nights I don't know *how* he got up. I knocked him out a couple of times.

I hit him one night in a playoff game at Olympia. We had some great series against Chicago. Holy Cripes. Mikita went down, and he didn't know what the hell was going on. He actually *crawled* to the bench. The next shift out, I hit him the same way. I mean, *I hit him.* You know when you've hit a guy playing hockey—it feels like a feather. But you know you hit him. He went down again. I went over the top of him and I said, "One of these days, you little bastard, you're not going to get up."

He flipped me off and said, "Screw you."

The little bastard never missed a shift. I'd nailed him twice that night. I'd hit him hard, twice, and they still beat us. As I'm coming out of the dressing room to meet my family I hear, "Hey, Bill."

I look over and there's Mikita.

He says, "If you want playoff tickets for the next round, call me."

I thought, "You little jerk."

He's the one guy in my career I think I hit more than anybody else. I didn't like him because the little bastard was dirty. He'd spear you in the back of the leg, your calf, going around the net. He'd chop you, hit you on the ankles, and spear you.

Sid Abel told me, the last year I played, "When Mikita comes over the red line your eyes get *this big!*"

I said, "Well, I'm looking for him, Sid. Every chance I get."

We had a lot of home-and-home games in those days with Toronto and Montreal. They come right on the same train, the same team that you played the night before, home-and-home. It's a wonder fights never broke out. Yeah, it's a wonder. Because I'll tell you, we've come close.

We used to walk through the cars and never say a word to them, most days. Go for breakfast or something. Never said a word. Once in a while, I'd say, "We'll see how tough you are tonight, you bastard." Things like that, and just keep walking.

I remember walking through cars there, and not even say a word—just look at those bastards. I didn't like them, anyway.

It's funny how that works. I got traded twice in my career, so I wound up playing with an awful lot of those guys.

First time I got dealt, it was to the New York Rangers from Chicago.

In New York, we had Andy Bathgate, Dean Prentice, Gump Worsley, Jack "Tex" Evans, Lou Fontinato, Camille Henry, and Parker MacDonald. Pretty good club.

Harry Howell and Lou Fontinato paired together on defense, so I paired up with Evans, who's passed away. He was good to work with.

We had a good power play in New York. Bathgate and myself, Dean Prentice, Camille Henry—you know Camille didn't weigh 130 pounds. He'd stay out after practice, and

Bathgate and I would shoot pucks. I've never seen a guy with his hands. Eight out of 10 he'd pick out of the air. He'd practice it. I've never seen a guy pick it like Camille. He'd drive the goaltenders crazy. If he scored 25 goals, 12 of them would be tipping in out of mid-air. He was uncanny, the little bastard. If you knocked him down, he was like a feather. He'd just kind of float down and get right back up. Camille Henry didn't weigh 135 pounds. But he was good with the puck, oh boy.

I played the point with Andy Bathgate in New York. Bathgate was one of the first slapshot guys. He could shoot the puck, boy. I used to feed him the puck all night long because he could really shoot it. He was very accurate. Bathgate and Bernie Geoffrion of Montreal were probably the first couple of guys who started the slapshot. Most people picked it up.

We never seemed to get over the top there. It always seemed to be a struggle the last month to get in the playoffs. We could never get over that hump in New York.

It was nice here when I came to Detroit. I didn't really care for New York that much. The management, they didn't seem to really care if you won or lost. They gave you that impression. I played there seven years, and we missed the playoffs four times.

General John Reed Kilpatrick owned the team. Muzz Patrick, Lester Patrick's son, was GM there. Phil Watson was coaching. *He* cared. Oooh, boy, he was something else. Then they brought in Alf Pike. Alf Pike. He played with the New York Rangers for many years in the '40s. Doug Harvey was coach of the Rangers after him, after we missed the playoffs three straight years. In Detroit, Jack Adams traded for me the month after Harvey got the job, so I never played for him.

Just to give you an example about New York: It's a zoo city, anyway; it's so big, and there are so many people. We had to live out on Long Island. Now, today's players, they're down in Manhattan. They got the money to buy the condos and apartments, or whatever.

They didn't seem to help you. New York? They had nothing. We just had to find a place on our own. We had six or seven players living in one complex on Long Island. Somebody found out about it, Harry Howell or Gump, and we had six or seven Rangers families living within half a mile.

When I came to Detroit, they had several homes that they had for you to look at. That makes a guy feel pretty good when he's coming to a city that he doesn't know. Makes you feel better. You get in a different mood, especially when you've got a family, you know? I had four daughters then, all seven or eight years old or under. You've got to have your family happy, or else it doesn't matter what you do, no matter what walk of life you're in.

But we were all right here. We've been here 34 years now. I got four daughters, and I got to tell you, they are something else. We got married in 1952. It's great, *great*! I got a good one, I'll tell you that, a good one. That's so important.

I met Edna in Edmonton. We were talking about it yesterday with the grandchildren. Went on and off with her for seven years. When I went pro, she figured that was it. I was going off to Chicago, and that would be the end of me.

It was tough on her, tough. Like I told you, we had four daughters. And every year, before we moved here, we'd ship three or four trunks of our belongings back east. She did it every fall. She had to do all that. It wasn't easy on the wives in those years. And most of the guys wanted to bring their families. A lot of them lived in the east. I lived in western Canada, quite a haul from out there.

So I'm signing my contract in New York. Muzz Patrick, he's the general manager—he's up in his office, and he showed me the contract. I'd just made the All-Star Team the year before, and it was a thousand-dollar raise, or something. Well, I wasn't too happy with that.

And I said, "Before we get into the contract, Muzz," I said, "my family is going to fly from Edmonton to New York, first class."

Oh, he threw his hands up in the air. "Holy Cow!" he said. "What did you say?"

"First class," I said. "I'm not even looking at the contract. I've got four daughters. It's tough on my wife. You've got to do something for them."

"Oh, no!" he said. "I can't start a thing like that. It would get around."

I said, "I'm not telling anybody. And if you don't tell anybody, nobody will know."

"No!" he says. "I got to check that out with General Kilpatrick!"

I said, "Well you better start checking now. I'm not even looking at this contract."

So the next day, I come to practice and he says, "I'm dead against it. Don't you tell *anybody*!"

I said, "I'm not going to tell anybody. Why the hell am I going to spread it around?"

They came first class the next few years. Which was a hell of a big difference, with four children.

Jack Adams traded for me and really treated me well after I got here. He gave me a raise and said, "I'll give you a two- or three-thousand-dollar bonus, just between you and me. If I think you've had a good year, you'll get it."

I made the second All-Star Team that year. We had our party after the season, and Jack walked in. We were up in the Alumni Room at Olympia.

Gordie said, "You got any bonuses coming?

I said, "Yeah, I do."

"He'll have them all in his pocket. Hope that your envelope is in his pocket," Gordie said.

So he went around, I saw Jack reach in and get this big thing with an elastic band around it,

and he's handing envelopes to different guys. Gordie and I are standing over in the corner, and here he comes.

Gordie said, "Either you or I are going to get something, because here he comes."

Sure as anything, he gives an envelope to each of us.

He shook my hand. He said, "You had a hell of a year."

There was three thousand bucks in there! Gee, that was big in the early '60s.

It's the most exciting time of the year, playoff time.

Sid Abel hated distractions, so during the playoffs, we'd stay at the Secor Hotel in Toledo. One game day, Pit Martin and Paul Henderson were sitting across from Gordie and me in the hotel dining room. They had great food there. Two or three in the afternoon of the game, they'd give us a big thick steak, New York strip, and a baked potato. Damn butterflies. Gordie and I couldn't eat it. We had poached eggs and toast.

I even got them the other day going to a Red Wings playoff game. Can you imagine that? Edna said, "What's the matter? You're not even talking."

"I got a few butterflies," I said. "I'm not even playing." As soon as I got in the rink, I was fine.

But we have played when we shouldn't have, when we were not fine. We got by, but it was a chore. Especially with bad charley horses or bad bruised hips. But once you get warmed up, you feel a lot better. You start sweating, and you feel all right.

In Toronto one night, in playoffs, a guy cross-checked me and tore my ribcage. I couldn't lift my arm. It was terrible, terrible. They wanted me to freeze it so I could still play. I asked the doctor if I got hit again, you know, could something serious happen.

"No way," he said. "They're torn so bad, you're going to have to wait until you're done with the season and let them heal."

When they get me in the hospital to freeze it up, I looked down and there were six needles sticking out of me. I didn't take another look.

You know when the freezing wore off? At the cottage in Edmonton, in June or July, that's when. I told the doctors about it. They didn't believe me. You could hit me in the ribs with a stick and I wouldn't even feel it—for two months. But I played. I played another six to eight games with it. Never felt it. The doctors here were good.

Everybody was good. The goalies were good. The best three goaltenders I've ever played with or against were Terry Sawchuk, Jacques Plante, and Glenn Hall. They were the best in my era, anyway. They were something else.

Sawchuk was a very different guy. I roomed with

him quite a bit when I played here in Detroit. He was a very moody guy. But he was one hell of a goalkeeper. He came to play. Just like a quarterback in football. Look at Arizona in the 2001 World Series, with Curt Schilling and Randy Johnson. I mean, they ruled the roost. It's the same in hockey. You got a hot goalkeeper, you can go a long way.

A lucky break can take you a long way, too. Remember in 1964? We were leading Toronto in the Stanley Cup Final, three games to two, and were playing Game 6 at Olympia. We could have won the Cup that night. That was the night Toronto defenseman Bobby Baun scored in overtime to beat us, after being carried off the ice on a stretcher in the third period, supposedly with a broken leg.

Baun got a lot of ink out of that. I keep telling him—I see him quite a bit—I always rib him about that. I said, "Boy, you got a lot of ink out of that thing. I didn't see you hobbling after the game." Whether it was broken or not, who cares?

About a minute before that goal was scored, we were in their end. We used to have a give-and-go play, we used to call it. Floyd Smith was the guy. I give it to him in the corner, and then break for the net. He gives me that pass right back. I shot the puck, and it's going into the top corner. Johnny Bower was the goalkeeper, and he's standing there frozen, and it hits the shaft of his stick, top part of the goal stick. It's going *exactly* in the top corner of the net! Bower never even saw it, and it hits the shaft of his stick and stays out. That puck goes in, and the

Detroit Red Wings win the 1964 Stanley Cup! Toronto came back a minute later and Bobby Baun scores the damn goal. True story.

So the series is tied, 3-3, instead of being over, and Toronto beats us in Game 7 at Maple Leaf Gardens.

In 1966, against Montreal in the Final, well, we got beat. We won the first two games—at The Forum, no less—but then the Canadiens beat us four in a row.

the boards, and that was it. They should've had replay. We'd have been all right; might have got new breath, new air. But that's the way it goes.

Henri Richard knows it was a bad goal. I've seen him in the last 10 or 15 years, lots of times, and he just kind of looks, smiles, and says something in French or something.

It always seemed to go the other way, not being on the Stanley Cup. Like I said, I played 20 years in the NHL. I was in Game 7 in the Final three or four times in my career. Or two or three.

"See, what happened—when the goal went in—the Montreal Canadiens, they just jumped over the boards, and that was it. They should've had replay. We'd have been all right; might have got new breath, new air. But that's the way it goes."

—BILL GADSBY

If they had a replay in those years, the winning goal in overtime in Game 6 wouldn't been counted, because Henri Richard put it in with his forearm! Gary Bergman had got him down on the ice, and they were sliding towards the net, and Richard just knocked it in. That was it.

I was on the bench at the time. I just know that it was a bad goal, because you could see it even from the bench that he put it in with his arm. I asked out goalie, Roger Crozier, and he said it was a bad goal.

See, what happened—when the goal went in— the Montreal Canadiens, they just jumped over

Against Toronto, Montreal, and it never come about. I always felt if I give it a good effort ... then it wasn't in the cards. If you give it a good effort and you play well—and you know when you've played good yourself, nobody has to tell you.

Now, when I come off the ice, I told Edna, "You've seen me play my last game. We're gonna retire and go home, honey. To Edmonton."

My mind and my body had had enough. That was it. It was the time to do it.

Edna said, "It's your life and your body. If you want to go home, we'll go home." I said, "Let's do it."

BENNY WOIT

"Bashin'"

Detroit Red Wings 1951-1955

Chicago Blackhawks 1955-1957

Stanley Cup 1952, 1954, 1955

I'll tell you about the train.

We're in the playoffs against Canadiens, and both our teams are going to Montreal for the next game. We were going into the dining car—the one that has all the seats along one side, like stools in a bar. We come in one at a time—Ted Lindsay and me and Gordie.

The Canadiens were in the car, and some of our guys were in the car, and we had to go by the Montreal players to get at where our guys were sitting. There wasn't much room.

Dickie Moore and Ted Lindsay almost had a big brawl right there that night. They both had to go by each other and they were just nose to nose.

And we were all standing there, Howe on one side and me on the other, and all the Montreal players stood up. Oh, jeez. My heart was just a-beating!

Finally they went by each other and that was it. They pretty much touched noses! That's how close it was! They went by and everybody said, "Oh, boy! *That* was nice."

The whole place would have been torn apart! They were a bad bunch, Montreal. I'd belonged to the Montreal organization for a year or two after that. They were no angels, either. They'd come after you. But it didn't bother us.

A lot of our guys didn't like the French Canadians, anyway. They always fought them. But it didn't matter. Marcel Pronovost and Johnny and

---

OPPOSITE: "Bashin'" Benny Woit takes a shot with a Bruins defender draped over him. (AP/WWP)

Larry Wilson were born there, too, in Quebec. They spoke better French than English when we first met them. Johnny can still *par le vous*.

I grew up in Thunder Bay, Ontario, on the North Shore of Lake Superior. That's right by Fort William, where Jack Adams is from. And Alex Delvecchio is from Fort William. We've had a few Hall of Fame guys from up there.

Do you think Jack went easier on us because we were both from his home town?

No. Heck, no! He was harder on us!

I get asked sometimes if I think we got the shaft when it came to money, and I always say the same thing: It was beautiful! *Beautiful!*

We used to go in to negotiate our contracts with Jack at Sault Ste. Marie, Michigan, in training camp.

One time we're all lined up, and Sawchuk was in Adams's office. All of a sudden the door opens. You could hear Adams yelling at Terry.

"Get out of here, you stupid Uke! You can talk when you feel right. Come back then. The hell with you!"

I was supposed to go in next, but Earl Johnson sneaked in ahead of me, and he went in there. Poor Earl stuttered sometimes.

The door was open and I could hear Earl. He sputtered, "Ah, ah, ah, ah…"

Adams yelled, "Say *something*, you son of a gun!"

But Adams couldn't get a word out of him. Adams got up, and he grabbed him and spun him around and kicked him in the rear end and whipped him out the door.

He shouted, "That's all I want to see today!"

I wish I had a camera that time. Did he ever give him a boot, right out the door!

Thank the Lord I didn't have to go in there.

You couldn't get *anything* off Adams. Nothing! He was almost as bad as Eddie Shore, and from what I've heard, Eddie Shore—the owner in Springfield in the American League—was the worst in hockey. Eddie Shore and him, Jack Adams, were on the same level for contracts. You couldn't get *a nickel* off him.

He picked on everyone. He picked on Lindsay, and he picked on Howe a little bit, too. He'd give them both the whole works.

I got to go to Red Wings training camp at Olympia when I was just a kid in the early 1940s, the war years. The first one I can still remember.

A couple of the old guys—Carl Liscombe and Howe—not Gordie Howe, the other Howe, Syd—they were on the one line. Liscombe and Howe, and I can't think of the other one; maybe it was Abel, one of those guys.

Oh, boy! I couldn't believe *anybody* could skate that fast and be that good! I was just, maybe

Benny Woit, whose head appears to be coming out of the Cup, was part of the Red Wings Stanley Cup winning team of 1951-52. (Courtesy of Robert L. Wimmer)

15. And I was playing defense, oh boy! They get you in your end and they were just *zooming* by you! Firing the puck! Oh, I couldn't believe it!

Growing up on the northern shore of Lake Superior, I'd never seen an NHL game player before, of course.

I'd never seen an NHL player either, but I saw our Senior team, the Port Arthur Bearcats, win the Allan Cup for best amateur team in all of Canada in 1939. We had Edgar Laprade! Edgar Laprade was a great, great hockey player for New York Rangers who's in the Hockey Hall of Fame now.

Edgar Laprade didn't turn pro until 1945, when he signed with the Rangers. He was 26 then, and all he did was go out and win the Calder Trophy for best rookie in the National Hockey League.

Edgar won the Lady Byng, too. The league gives that out for Most Gentlemanly Player. The year he won it, 1949-50, Edgar Laprade didn't get a single penalty. Not one! Zero penalty minutes in 60 games!

Teddy Lindsay just nailed him this one time. You know, I still remember when he hit him. Oh, jeez, the blood all over the place.

That's the only guy Ted Lindsay ever went back to and said he was sorry. He kind of looked at Edgar and he almost apologized. But I don't think he did. Pretty close, yes.

Lindsay was a mean little son of a gun. You couldn't get too close to him or you were bleeding. He was a tough little son of a gun. He fought a lot of them, and he won a lot of them. He lost a few, too.

Teddy was hated by everyone he played against, sure. *And* by his *own* players sometimes, too! Everybody! We had to practice against him, don't forget. Certainly, he'd give it to you in practice. It didn't matter.

Tough guys? There were lots of them. There was a guy named John Mariucci, who played for Chicago. Mariucci wasn't that big of a man, but he was a mean little son of a gun, too.

There was a Red Wings defenseman Mariucci hit in the back of the head. He woke up on the train going home. I've been trying to think of his name for a long time. Doug McCaig! I've been trying to think of that darn name for years now. Big man. He was a big man and a tough son of a gun. Oh boy, Doug McCaig. He'd nail you.

Mariucci hit him in the back of the head. He never saw him coming. Doug McCaig was out. On the train, he didn't know where the hell he was, he didn't know what happened.

Later, he remembered and he was going to go back and kill him again. Doug McCaig, you son of a gun! Beautiful!

Anyhow, I just missed getting to play against Edgar when the Rangers played Detroit for the Stanley Cup in 1950. That was the year before I joined the Red Wings, which was the spring of 1951 when I was 22. They called me up for two games in Detroit, in March.

They kept me around for the 1951 playoffs. We were the defending champs, Detroit, but that was when Rocket Richard scored in the fourth overtime in Game 1 of the semifinals at Olympia. And two nights later, the Rocket scored in the third overtime in Game 2. The final score that night was 1-0. Those were the first two playoff games Terry Sawchuk ever played in.

So we lost two in overtime at Olympia to start the best-of-seven series, and we had to go to Montreal for the next two. We lost to the Canadiens in six games in '51.

The next year, 1951-52, I made the Detroit team and played in 58 of the 70 regular-season games and in all eight playoff games. *And we won each and every one of those playoff games.*

Wasn't that something? 1952.

Terry got four shutouts in the playoffs. We didn't get scored on at Olympia Stadium in the entire playoffs! Detroit outscored the Maple Leafs and Canadiens, 10-0, at Olympia in the four playoff games there that year. We were the first team ever to win the Stanley Cup in an eight-game sweep.

Like I said: Wasn't that something? 1952!

That's the first year I was up for the whole season. We had Bob Goldham, Red Kelly, Leo Reise and Marcel Pronovost on defense.

But in the playoffs, Red Kelly got hurt; broke his hand. And Leo Reise got hurt; he had a bad knee or something.

So that left just the three of us. Our coach, Tommy Ivan, didn't put anybody else out there. They dressed Red Kelly, broken hand and all, for three of the four games, but Goldham and I and Pronovost played pretty much the whole Final against Montreal.

In Montreal, I remember, the whole club went out the night before. Everybody went out. We went to see Dorothy Lamour, who was singing at a nightclub. I had a couple of beers and I went home early. And who do I run into right at the desk? Tommy Ivan—our coach. He says to me, "That's it! You're going to be out there all the time! And don't you let them score!"

At the morning skate, we'd usually just practice a little bit and then get off the ice. Because it's a game day, you take it easy, a little—especially because we've only got three defensemen. The guys are all hurt.

But that day, Tommy Ivan had another whole practice with all the guys that they brought up extra from the American League. And Ivan kept me out there with 'em.

And then the game that night: Game 1 of the 1952 Stanley Cup Final at The Forum in Montreal.

We were playing in the third period; we're leading Montreal, 2-1. I come off. I'm ready to take my turn off because there's only three of us who are changing: Pronovost, Goldham and me.

And no! Tommy Ivan said, "Get back out there! *And if they score, you're going to get it!*"

And they didn't.

We beat them, yeah. Oh, boy, that was really something. They were never *near* our end! That damn Rocket there, he was just a-flyin' all the time. And the Rocket could let 'er go. He was a son of a gun. He was great.

The Rocket was flying around, and all and we were *eating that puck!* Only three of us defensemen, and we beat them anyway!

We had such great players. Gordie Howe and I roomed together in 1940-something for one week, in training camp beside the Olympia there. He probably doesn't even remember that we roomed together.

And then he went to Omaha or somewhere. I went to St. Michael's to play Junior in Toronto.

Gordie was powerful then. He could skate and he could shoot. He could do everything. You could tell he was going to be a dandy, the best at everything. He had everything. And Gordie was tough. Nobody wanted to bother too much with him. Yes, they kept away from him.

And a great guy, too. They didn't come much better. In the room he was quiet. He'd always fool around. He'd grab you by the neck and lift you right up. Or he'd give you a little shot; hit you with a fist on the side of the head or somewhere. Pretty near knock you right out. Gordie was just playing, yeah.

We give it back to him, too. He used to get some, but not too often.

Marcel Bonin was a powerful man, real powerful. Gordie and him were having a shower, and I happened to peek in there.

I said, "Gordie, why don't you take care of *him* yourself?"

Howe grabbed Bonin by the neck, *one hand*, and he lifted him right up. Bonin's hanging onto the pipes so hard he pretty near burned his hand. Gordie stretched Marcel's neck out quite a bit!

Bonin said, "Boy, he's strong, man."

I said, "Yeah!"

I was Sawchuk's roommate. We were good buddies. We were close, real close. There weren't many in hockey who can say they were close with Sawchuk, no. He had his ways.

But he was a good guy. If they scored a goal on him, he'd say, "That's all they're getting. Get two and we'll win it. We're going to win it."

I still don't think there's anybody close to him.

I don't know what set him apart. Did you know that elbow of his was always bent? He broke it playing baseball, and he got run over by a car, too.

He used to hang on to the bumper on cars in the wintertime when he was a kid. Once, he put his tongue on it and it froze, and he was stuck, and he couldn't let go. He finally let go and it took part of his tongue off. Worse, then he got run over by another car. So his arm was crooked as hell there. We used to always kid him.

He was in that deal to Boston after he won the Cup in Detroit in 1955. He was sick about that one. Terry had a nervous breakdown, I think. We were in Chicago, and every time we played them, we'd go out and he'd say, "Gee, I don't know if I can do it anymore. I gotta quit."

I'd say, "You're crazy. You're still the best." It took him a year or two, and he got over it.

A great guy, Terry. We miss him so much, son of a gun.

Terry was coming over to see us the spring he died, when he was only 40. It was May 1970.

We saw each other quite often. Right before he died, he called and said, "I'm coming down for a week or two to your place. Make sure you're ready."

But, boom. He was gone. I couldn't believe it; couldn't believe it.

When I was thinking about him, it was funny. One of the things I remembered was this one time—must have been the only time—he made me look bad. In the playoffs against Montreal, Terry—on a shot from outside the blue line—missed it. Probably the only goal he missed all his life.

Did I ever get it for that one. Adams was giving me hell: "You stupid son of a gun!" He'd use some pretty rough language.

But here's the thing: Jack Adams, he couldn't see too well. In fact, he couldn't see *anything*. Our bench where we started the game, he could see that end pretty good. The other side, he could see hardly at all.

He didn't know what the heck was going on!

You'd be sitting on the bench beside Sid Abel, and all of a sudden you'd hear Jack start yelling at one of the guys on the ice.

"Benny! What are you doing! Why did you do that!"

Sid would lean over to me and say, "Did you get all of that?"

Jack was missing a pretty good show. Some of the guys could shoot pretty good in our day. Howe could let 'er go pretty good. Lindsay, too.

Jack and Lindsay didn't hit it off near the end. At the outset, Jack loved him.

And Teddy just loved Gordie, and Gordie just loved him, too. I don't know whether they're talking to each other now—Teddy and Gordie—but it's hard to believe if they aren't, because for years and years, if you saw one, you saw the other. Within two feet, anyway. They always drove in the same car to training camp. Everything! Oh, boy.

And now, they don't. It's unbelievable! It's sickening. I can't believe it! I just can't believe it!

We had some great times. Those were good, good times. The memories are very nice. We were right together. We did everything together. Lindsay was the first guy to buy a house, so we would go to his home. We were all over there helping him, right. We were right together. It all feels like yesterday.

Now we're all starting to limp. We're getting a little gray, and our faces are sewn up bad. The stitching wasn't done real good.

How do I want to be remembered? Oh, I don't know. Just as honest; underpaid and honest. We were all that way, anyway.

JOHNNY WILSON

"IRON MAN"
DETROIT RED WINGS 1950-1955; 1957-1959
CHICAGO BLACKHAWKS 1955-1957
TORONTO MAPLE LEAFS 1959-1961
NEW YORK RANGERS 1961-1962
STANLEY CUP 1950, 1952, 1954, 1955

I WAS BORN IN KINCARDINE, Ontario, but I was raised in Shawinigan Falls, Quebec, where I grew up with my younger brother, Larry, Marcel Pronovost, Jacques Plante, and Jean Guy Talbot. Larry, Marcel and I played in Detroit. Those other guys went to the Canadiens.

We played hockey in the winter and baseball in the summer. Jacques Plante was the catcher and I was the pitcher on the same baseball team in our juvenile league. That's why I understood when Plante became the first goalie who started wearing a mask with Montreal in 1959. He was a catcher. He was used to having the mask on. He thought that was great. To him, it made perfect sense!

Growing up, the war was on and we didn't have money. I was trying to make a few bucks to give to my mother and father. I was working at the high school during the off season, 15, 16 years old, helping the janitor. My brother was working for the A&P supermarket.

One day, Jack Adams and Tommy Ivan, the general manager and the coach of the Detroit Red Wings, came in on a little cruise. Just to meet some of the players.

Everybody in Shawinigan Falls was going, "Wow, Jack Adams and Tommy Ivan!" Everybody was talking. They came to the high school to meet me and they went to the A&P store and brought my brother out of the back, where he was unloading stock, and they met him there.

That's how we were originally scouted. When I was 17 years old I signed what they called a "B" form. We got, I think, $500 apiece for signing. The "B" Form gave Detroit, according to the wording, "an exclusive option on our services a hockey player." So here we are: we're tied up with the Red Wings for eternity. That was the system.

Then they sent us a pair of skates and a couple of sticks. We *never* had new skates in those days. Our parents couldn't afford it. Here you are, just a young puppy dog, so to speak, and wow, you're with the Red Wings! 16, 17 years old! You cherish the idea!

Oh, I enjoyed playing! I never missed a game! I was the "Iron Horse" of hockey, that's right.

In fact, they called me "Iron Man," because from the final 20 games of 1952 with Detroit, until the fall of 1960 when I was a Maple Leaf, I didn't miss a single game: eight seasons in a row where I played in all 70 games for 560 straight, plus those 20 games at the end of '52. 580 games in a row; an NHL record until Andy Hebenton of the Rangers broke it a few years later.

It didn't end—the streak, that is—because I got hurt.

What happened was, when I was with Toronto, we got into a little contractual dispute with the coach and general manager Punch Imlach—me and several other guys.

We wanted more money, but in those days they handled money like it was bark on a tree. They were tight. Airtight. Raises were not that prominent, even though we had played the Canadiens

Johnny Wilson (Courtesy of Robert L. Wimmer)

in the Stanley Cup Finals the previous spring and lost in six games.

As a result of wanting more money, we hemmed and hawed all through training camp, and six of us didn't go to Montreal where the opening game was.

Montreal blew them out. I think it was 6-1. The next night Toronto goes into Boston, and Boston beats them. Naturally, that week when they came back, Punch started to sympathize with us a little bit and give us a few more dollars. That's when we signed our contract and ended up playing.

But that's how I lost my consecutive game streak—those two games to start the season in 1960.

I remember so many games in Olympia; in all those Original Six buildings. It was fabulous. In my era—in every rink with the exception of Chicago—you left the dressing room and you walked through the crowd to the ice.

Now the players are sheltered from the fans. They've got tunnels they go through, so the fans can't get to them.

We'd walk out of our dressing room into the lobby. There were guardrails, but you were walking right in the middle of the fans. They'd pat you on the back as you were walking—you know, kind of fire you up.

When you appeared out on the ice, the fans would start to roar. Of course, playing for a winning club was gratifying, because the fans were into it, and we were sold out every night.

We didn't have any glass or mesh behind our bench. The fans would lean on the back of our bench. They could talk to the players before they went out on the ice.

One night I'm sitting next to Ted Lindsay, and we were shuffling down the bench because we had only one gate in those days.

Teddy was really harassing the referee, really giving it to him. Some of the words that came out of his mouth! Off the ice, Teddy was a very gentle person, but when he got near the ice, *nobody* was his friend.

He was on this referee, and I looked behind me and there was this couple I knew.

Teddy was really ripping this referee and she's poking Teddy in the ribs shouting, "You give it to him, Teddy! You give it to him!"

So I'm thinking, "Wow, she's *really* getting into it!"

But that's how close the fans were to you. When I first broke in, they didn't have any glass around the boards. Instead of glass they used chicken wire, steel mesh. When we had the mesh, you could hear fans yelling. Going in the corners, you could hear them yelling at you as you were playing.

Some of the fans, they'd get fired up and they'd spit at you; they'd push some stuff through the mesh and do things that would irritate you. They'd call you different names when you were crushed up against the boards. "You're a bully," or "You've got no guts!" You could hear them yelling when you were playing. Then they put the glass there and you couldn't hear *anything*.

Here's another thing about that mesh. In practice occasionally, when you'd go in the corner with Gordie Howe, all of a sudden he'd get that big hand out and he'd *play* with you. If you had your head down looking for the puck, he'd push

From left: Gordie Howe, Marcel Bonin, Glen Skove, Johnny Wilson, and Marty Pavelich. The "suit" is Jimmy Skinner. (Courtesy of Robert L. Wimmer)

your face into that mesh. He wouldn't deliberately hurt you; he'd just give you a little push. For a while your face was a little marked up from the mesh.

Gordie liked to have a few laughs, and later he'd say, "Hey, John, your face looks a little funny. You've got it all marked up like that." He'd laugh.

If you were backchecking in practice he'd get you under the arm with his stick and pull you back. He says, "You're going too fast. Come on back here a little bit." Stuff like that. He got a

kick out of it. It would agitate you, but what could you say? Good teammate, yeah.

I used to scrimmage against Gordie Howe. He was a right wing and I was a left wing, see?

Well, I'd beat Gordie occasionally. So playing *against* Gordie in practice, I got confidence. You were practicing against the best right winger in hockey, so if you'd beat him from time to time, or make a play, you'd say, "Wow! I did it to Gordie—the best! Why can't I do it against anybody else in the league?"

The first time I saw Gordie play was at training camp in 1947. I was hoping to make the Windsor Spitfires team, which we did—Marcel Pronovost, my brother, Larry, and I. I was 18.

That winter, we had access to the Olympia. When the Spitfires didn't play, we'd come over and watch the Red Wings play. We'd get in for free because we had a pass; we'd get in the back door. We were in Standing Room, and after the game we'd come down with the fans and jump on the Grand River bus to take you downtown, then take the tunnel bus back to Windsor, go home and go to school the next day.

Junior hockey players today, they have cars. We had to take the tunnel bus, walk into Detroit, and take the Grand River bus all the way up to the Olympia.

Jimmy Skinner was our coach at the time in Windsor. Jimmy was like a father to me. He was so good. He was there all the time, and if you'd have some problems, he'd talk to you.

He taught me a lot about hockey. In those days, we didn't have much coaching. The game, you more or less taught yourself. They didn't refine the power play. They didn't refine forechecking. You made the team simply because you were a good hockey player. But Jimmy could whip you pretty good. Just because you're a junior hockey player, either you'd produce or you wouldn't be around.

Jimmy was the only one who had a car. If some of the guys wanted to go to the hockey game, he'd meet at the Windsor Arena, and you'd get in the car and drive over. So that would save you going over by bus.

We used to go to quite a few of the games. My idol was Teddy because I was a left winger. I learned a lot from watching Teddy play. There was no TV. We saw pictures in the paper, and that was the extent of it. You can't learn much from a still photograph. So, I used to watch what Teddy did out on the ice. Then, I'd do the same thing in my junior games in Windsor.

Now, kids can watch hockey on TV and establish an idol and watch his moves out there. Then they can go through those moves the next day on the ice. We couldn't do that until we actually saw them with our own eyes.

Teddy was a good two-way hockey player. He was rugged in the corners. Teddy said to me, "Johnny, when you play in this league, when you make passes, don't stand there and admire your pass. Make the play and get that stick up, because somebody's going to hit you. If you keep your stick up, the guy is going to have to go through your stick to get to you."

I learned right away that Teddy was right. The very first game I played I went in the corner and Fleming Mackell of Toronto high-sticked me. It was an accidental deal where he flipped me on my back and his stick caught me in the mouth and knocked two of my teeth out.

I learned from that. You've got to keep that stick up when you pass. That's one of the things I learned from Teddy. You have to keep your stick up, because if not, you'll end up with a lot more stitches than you think.

Teddy knew how to handle himself. I learned that from him. He was one of the best captains I played for. He could get you fired up for a game. He hated the opposition.

Both of those guys, Teddy and Gordie, at that time were single, so they used to come over and watch the Spitfires play. Then they'd come up to the dressing room. Well, we thought that was *great*, having the Red Wings come by.

I mean, it would give us inspiration to go out there and play hard, knowing that these Red Wings were looking at us. Hopefully, one day we'd be able to play with them.

That's what happened; you developed within the organization and along the way, you end up getting to know them really well.

Gordie was just coming into his own then. You could see he was overpowering the Rocket. The Rocket was the big number-one star, and you could see where Gordie was starting to come along and overpower him—and the league.

He could handle the puck and get it on the net. In the corners, he'd always come up with the puck and make great plays. He was all-around; he could check, he could stickhandle, he could shoot, he could switch hands, he could fight.

I mean, if there was *anyone* in hockey that you would think would be the complete player, it was him!

Nobody disturbed Gordie, because if he got mad, I mean, *look out*—somebody's going to start flying around there.

We were safe with him on the ice. No team was ever going to come over and beat *us* up, because we had our ace in the hole: Gordie. See?

Let me ask you this. How many times will the outstanding player on your team be the best fighter on your team, the best goal scorer on your team, the toughest on your team, the toughest in the corners on your team? Know what I mean? He's one of a kind! There's no way *anybody* can top Gordie Howe!

I don't think, as a coach, that you could say to Wayne Gretzky, "I want you to go and slap so-and-so around because if you get to him tonight, we're going to win the game. He's the best player on Boston." You can go down the roster even today. Mario Lemieux—you couldn't say to Mario, "We're going have a tough game tonight, Mario. You've got to start nailing that so-and-so over there; he's their best player."

No. Gretzky wouldn't have it; Lemieux wouldn't have it; Bobby Hull, Jean Beliveau, the same way.

Gordie wouldn't hesitate!

He'd start banging guys, and nobody would get *near* him. Adams wouldn't tell him to do it, but Gordie had a good feel for the game. We'd have our morning meetings and we'd pretty well know who we might be playing against, and Gordie would say, "Don't worry. I'll look after my guy."

If you had to fight to win a game, if you had a crash the guy into the boards to win a game, if you had to intimidate a guy with a little elbow

From left: Gordie Howe, Johnny Wilson, Norm Ullman, Marcel Pronovost, and Terry Sawchuk. (Courtesy of Robert L. Wimmer)

or a crosscheck, or whatever, Gordie would do it.

You wouldn't see that from the likes of Gretzky or Lemieux—to go out and actually try and bait a guy into a fight.

Gordie could score goals, he backchecked, he blocked shots; I mean, you name it, he did it all.

Having Gordie Howe was like having six players on the ice. He could do the job of two. He'd backcheck and defensively he'd get the puck and work it out of his own end. Nobody could get it from him. Offensively, Gordie was so strong, so tough to knock off his skates. He could ward you off with one arm and still maintain control of that puck. He was strong enough that he could push guys aside. He was exceptional.

Plus, he was a great guy. Good sense of humor.

After we won the Stanley Cup one year, Al Philpot—a great hockey fan—he owned a big house and a big boat down on the Inter-Coastal Waterway down by Miami and Metro Prystai and I went down there on the spur of the moment.

After winning the Cup, we went out and did a little partying, and Metro says, "We've been invited. Let's get in the car and go to Florida."

"What an idea!" I said.

So, here we are, 21 years old, whatever, we go to Florida, and we get down there and we're staying at the same motel with Teddy and Gordie. Now Philpot says, "C'mon. We'll all meet tomorrow morning and we'll go deep-sea fishing."

So we all met—Gordie, Teddy, Metro and me—down at Al's dock. Of course, Metro and I had been out partying. Gordie and Teddy were married, so they stayed in. Metro and I got in about 1 o'clock in the morning. We had to get up at 5 to go fishing.

So we get on the boat and away we go. We're out there in the ocean, and Teddy and Gordie are way up on top in the crow's nest deep-sea fishing.

Meantime, a storm comes in. And the barracudas are following our boat, and we're going up and down with the waves. Teddy and Gordie are up there fishing, and Al said, "You better get down here!"

Metro and I are down below, and all of a sudden, Metro went white as a sheet. He got a little seasick. He didn't know what to do.

We're going up and down, and Al's on the radio calling in a mayday, "We're lost. Where are we?"

I want to tell you something, it was damn scary, especially when he was calling in that mayday on the ship-to-shore radio! We didn't know where the hell we were! I thought the boat was going to capsize. I was in fear for my life. Yes I was! We were going up and down on these huge waves, and the barracudas were following our boat! You could see them!

Jack Adams would have had a heart attack if he'd known.

And Gordie is up there *laughing*. He didn't give a damn! Gordie is up there, "Look at that one jump out of the water!" You know Gordie.

Of course, we're all young guys. We had no fear in those days.

Finally, the storm subsided, and we made our way back to the dock. Metro got off and he kissed the dock.

I said to Metro later, "Imagine if that boat *had* gone over—a Stanley Cup team losing four of their players in one shot?" To this day, Jack, he never knew about it.

That was all during the Stanley Cup days. It was fun.

We had another close call, too. We were going to play at the Forum. Gordie, Teddy, my brother and I are in a cab. On the way to the Forum some guy ran a red light and the cabbie slammed on his brakes. We almost got killed, broad-sided. I'm thinking, "There are two All-Stars in the back there. If something would have happened, it would have been a disaster. If we'd have got nailed, which could have happened, we would have had two of the greatest players in hockey dead in the back seat!

That was in '52, when we won the Stanley Cup; when we won eight straight in the playoffs. That was amazing. The greatest achievement in life is to win the Stanley Cup. You win the individual award, it's kind of nice. It's more gratifying to win the Cup! Some players play all their careers, never to be on a Stanley Cup team. The Cup is one of the most cherished pieces of silverware existing today because your names appear on the cup. There's no other trophy where they put your name on it.

It was a little different when you won in those days. Our celebration was from center ice to the dressing room. Jack Adams would lock the door for 10 or 20 minutes and he'd finally let the media in with their cameras and everything else. Then he'd take the Cup down to the Book Cadillac Hotel downtown. He'd have it on display at the team party that night for the family and friends who were there with you, and that's the last time you saw it. Until you won it again. Now today they carry it all over the place. Which is nice.

A lot of things were different then, of course. In those days, we paid for parking. No free parking; we parked in different lots around Olympia. They wouldn't pay for your parking!

Now, the players have *valet parking*. Sure, the guys must tip the valet parking attendants, but we would have liked to have had that privilege, too. But we had to park across the street. Some of the guys walked to the rink because they lived in homes right around the Olympia.

Marcel Pronovost and a lot of us lived in Windsor. So we used to cross the border all the time. There's another toll that we had to pay. We'd come over twice a day. The day of the game, we'd come over for a meeting. We'd never skate the day of the game, but we would have a meeting. So it was a buck to come over in the morning and a buck to go back, and a buck to come over for the game that night and a buck to go back after that. It kind of adds up, you know?

When I was in New York City playing for the Rangers, we lived on Long Island. It was a buck-and-a-quarter an hour for a babysitter. If we played a 7:30 game, we had to leave at 4 o'clock. We had a good hour-and-twenty-minute commute. If we took the Van Wyck Freeway, you had to go over two bridges and through two tunnels. So that would cost us between $2 and $3 each way, then you had to pay $5 to park next to the Madison Square Garden.

I figured it out one time. It was costing me $25 to go play a game! Out of my pocket! To go and play! It's like paying to go to work. You know, "Here's 25 bucks. Now can I start work?"

When we first started in the '50s, meal money was $8 a day. You could have breakfast for 75 cents, lunch for a buck and a half, dinner for about $4.50. You could have a nice steak. If you wanted beers after the game, either you starve at lunch to save a few bucks, or you cut back on your dinner, you know?

We had a good hockey club. We had a good line. Alex Delvecchio, Metro Prystai and I, we clicked together. In Detroit, the second and third line, regardless of who you were, had to be checkers. We took the pressure off the big line. We used to come through and beat Rocket Richard or whoever we were supposed to check on the other teams' top line.

Gordie and Teddy, on the big line, had the privilege of springing loose a little more. They were supposed to score, but we scored big goals too, Alex and Metro and me. Tony Leswick and Marty Pavelich, they all got key goals. One year, 1954, Gordie got 33 goals, Teddy got 26, and I was next in line with 17. So, as a plus, our checking lines would get some key goals.

We never juggled lines in those days. I think it was better. It was Gordie and Teddy and Sid Abel for years, and then it was Gordie, Teddy and Earl Reibel. Glen Skov, Tony Leswick and Marty Pavelich were a line and then there was Metro, Alex and I. It was good and I'll tell you why. Take Delvecchio. You're playing with the guy so much I knew Alex's habits; what he was going to do. And he knew when I was going to break, where I'd get the puck. He pretty well knew my timing because we practiced together. And I knew with Prystai or Billy Dineen or whoever I was playing with basically what he'd do once he got to the blue line. We knew one another, you know?

Today the game is all this forechecking; dump it in, fire it around the glass. We never fired it around the glass. We thought that was a waste of time. Unless you passed it on a guy's stick, the guy wasn't too happy.

Another thing I notice today as opposed to when we played, a lot of the players hit with their elbows and arms up. And they hit from behind! They're crashing guys in the boards from behind and it's dangerous! I don't see any reason to do that.

Our main objective when we went in the corner was to get the puck! We were supposed to go in the corner and try to push the defenseman aside, not necessarily run him into the boards. If you check a guy from behind, once you release your weight you can't get the puck, because you're going with the guy into the boards. By the time you get stable on your feet to get the puck, it's gone! Our objective was to wedge a guy into the boards, let the boards do the work, where he couldn't keep control of the puck and you'd get it and make your play or your teammate will come in as a tandem to pick up the loose puck. That's what we used to do. They don't do that now. Now these guys are so mean they want to crash the guy against the boards.

If Jack Adams saw the way they play hockey today, he'd probably have a heart attack.

Take that move Steve Yzerman makes where he goes hard into the offensive zone, then stops, usually in or near the circles, and spins to shake the defense. If Adams saw that he'd have a heart attack! Once you got in that area from the top of the circles where Steve is, you *had* to shoot the puck at the net! Fire it at the net! Make the goaltender make a save.

If you passed it around more than twice, you might never play another game with Detroit! It was one or two passes and then right at the net. Don't dilly-dally, don't try to stick handle through, shoot it at the net.

Jack put the pressure on you all the time. Shoot the puck in, chase the puck. Make quick passes, drive the net. He wanted you to go for the net if you were a winger. He wanted the other guy to shoot it so you could go for the rebound.

At the Olympia, Jack sat behind our bench in a box with railings and a steel gate. At the end of a period if we heard a big clang—that gate slamming, we knew *somebody* was going to get it. You knew he wasn't too happy with what was going on down there.

I remember one night Alex and I were having a tough time getting out of our own end. We were rookies. We're in the dressing room and we've got our heads in our knees. We're bent over and then all of a sudden we see shoes in front of us on the floor. Jack was pigeon-toed, so there was no doubt about who was standing over us. He had clenched his fists.

"If you passed it around more than twice, you might never play another game with Detroit!"

—JOHNNY WILSON

The defensemen stayed up. They didn't want the opposition to take the blue line. If Jack ever saw a defenseman fall back like they do today, the way they collapse and give you the blue line, you might be in places he used to call Oshkosh or Kookamunga or somewhere.

Jack was a tough man to play for. He was fair, but he was all for the team. He kept you on your toes. Say you played a bad game the night before and he saw you in the hallway. He wouldn't say *anything*. It would be like he was growling. He'd walk by you like you were nobody. But if you played a good game, he'd come over and he'd put his fist on your chin, "Atta boy, son. You played a great game!"

Adams looked at Alex and me and he says, "I don't know what kind of game you guys are playing out there, but it's not hockey! You better get your act together or you won't be around *here* too long! I'll send you so far away a *carrier pigeon* couldn't find you."

That was a little warning that you might be in the minor leagues if you didn't pick it up. That's the way he was. He couldn't care less who it was. If you're not going to play well, you're gone.

Needless to say, we hit that second period like somebody shot us out of a cannon. I mean, I don't think the opposition touched the puck.

Jack was a different general manager. Tommy Ivan coached, but Jack would go in and overpower the coach. If you lost two in a row he'd get frustrated. He'd come down and yell at the team. If I were the coach, I wouldn't want a manager to come and interfere with my game plan or with my association with the team.

Tommy used to come in after Jack Adams would rattle our brains, so to speak. Jack used to come in at meetings and give a guy grief, and Tommy would sit there and wait until Jack took off. Then Ivan would say, "Do it this way until the old man leaves the building."

He'd be that kind of guy. He wouldn't let you get on edge just because Jack was mad. Tommy Ivan was good for the team. He knew he had a good hockey team. He didn't agitate anybody. He let you play your own game.

Tommy eventually took off and went to Chicago when he had a chance to be manager and coach.

For training camp every year, we'd all go off to Sault Ste Marie. We were up there for maybe five weeks. After were there for a week, Adams used to say, "All right, hang around the hotel. I'm going to start to sign you guys to one-year contracts." And do you know what? Within one week's time he'd have all 150 hockey players signed.

He'd say, "Okay, Johnny. It's your turn."

Man, you'd be there in about 10 minutes. You'd expect to argue about your contract.

He'd already have it all typed up.

He'd say, "You had a pretty good year, son. What kind of money are you looking for?"

I'd say, "I think a raise of $1000; maybe $1,500 would be about right."

He'd have you penciled in for $500.

He'd say, "Where do you want to play? Detroit? Indianapolis? Omaha?"

I'd say, "Where's the pen?" He'd broom you out in 10 minutes.

He was a beauty.

You had no other alternative. Today, the players have got it made. They've signed a contract and it's binding for one year, two years, or three years. And plus they've got their farm team sitting in the press box. They've got 25 guys here all the time. We had the maximum, 17. And we played a lot of times hurt. Unless you had a fracture, you played.

You had to make the team every year, whether you had a good year or a bad year. Except for Howe, Lindsay and guys like that. There was always somebody knocking on your door for your job. So you were pressurized from the time you joined the club every fall to when you won the Stanley Cup to when you went to training camp the next year. You still had to play for your job.

In 1954 we won the Stanley Cup. At that time

we got $3,000 to win the Stanley Cup. Players today, I don't know what their playoff bonus is, but it's a hell of a lot more than $3,000. Of course, we never thought we'd see the day where you end up paying $450 for a ticket to see a hockey game in the playoffs.

All the other times we won the Cup we got that $3,000. Taxes would take out about $300. So you'd end up with $2,700.

In '54, we ended up with $2,100.

When we went to training camp the next year, Ted Lindsay said, "I don't know about you guys, but all I got for my playoff bonus was $2,100.

We said, "That's all we got, too."

So, he stuck his nose out and went to see Jack Adams to see what happened, since he was the captain of the team.

Adams's response was that we had 17 players, two trainers, an assistant trainer, a coach.

Well, by the time the Teddy Lindsay finished talking to him, it wasn't 20 people who got all of the playoff shares—it was 28 or 29!

Teddy says to Jack, "How'd you come up with 29?"

"Well, the box office manager was a contributor," Adams said. "The chief scout, the head electrician..."

And he went on and on and on until he had about 28 or 29. That's why we end up with $2,100.

That's when the Players Association started.

Ted Lindsay is the guy who spearheaded the whole association. Teddy had all the little goodies. He was a great inspiration to Gordie and all the guys on the team. He was the *first* guy to stick up for his team. He didn't care if it was against the referees, or management, or the league.

He hated the opposition, but when the Association started, he stuck his nose out. He hated guys like Doug Harvey. He hated Jimmy Thomson, even though he played with him at St. Mikes. He hated Fernie Flaman. He hated *all* the guys he played against. It used to break his heart because he had to go and talk to these guys to put the Association together. He didn't like that.

In our era, we did not socialize with other players. Because we were drafted by the parent club and we stayed with the parent club.

Nowadays you and I might be playing for the Windsor Spitfires and we'd be buddies and roommates. All of a sudden you get drafted by Chicago and I'm drafted by Detroit.

So, on the ice I might say I can't hit you because we're buddies. There's a little bit of that going on today, because friendships are there.

What we did was, we contributed $100 apiece to get the NHL Players Association launched. We were supposed to sign this petition down the road to make it official.

Jack must've talked to Gordie.

Gordie said, "I'm not signing."

Red Kelly said, "I don't believe in unions."

So, nobody on our club signed it.

As a result, we didn't have an Association.

What we were trying to do was, once we had the Association together, we would probably be able to negotiate a lot better than the individual going in on his own. If there were any problems in terms of playoff money, bonuses; whatever benefits at that particular time we were in search of—we'd be better off addressing them as a group.

Go in as an individual and they could send you to the minors overnight. They'd just say, "Hey, if you don't like it here Johnny, see you later. Take the train to Indianapolis."

So, what we did is we kept our mouths shut.

Jack was noted as a trader. Two months after we won the Cup in 1955, Jack made a few deals. Four of the guys—Terry Sawchuk, Marcel Bonin, Lorne Davis, and Vic Stasiuk went to Boston. Four of us went to Chicago.

I was one of the guys who went to Chicago. I found out on the radio driving home from playing golf or something. I heard that I'd been traded to Chicago along with Glenn Skov, Benny Woit, and Tony Leswick. It broke my heart, because we all grew up together as Red Wings.

I was angry at Jack, sure. I was disturbed because number one, my heart and soul was with the Red Wings. Even today, even though I played with Chicago and Toronto and New York, my heart is still with the Wings.

Team chemistry, that's what he destroyed. Adams destroyed it. We were a team. We were Detroit Red Wings! We lived and died with one another! We helped each other. We stood up for one another. If one of us was going bad, we'd put our heads together, have a meeting to see if there wasn't something we could come up with to help the guy out.

A team misses that. That's what he destroyed. And then the Wings never won the Stanley Cup again until 1997. Over 40 years and they never won the Cup.

Well, these are the things that cross your mind; some of the things that you feel proud of. Nobody goes around bragging about their careers. How great they played. They talk more that it was a privilege to play in the National Hockey League and to be associated with and involved in hockey. These are things that are living memories. You think back about the fun you had in your career.

LEONARD "RED" PATRICK KELLY

"RED"

DETROIT RED WINGS 1947-60

TORONTO MAPLE LEAFS 1960-67

STANLEY CUP, 1950, 1952, 1954, 1955, 1962, 1963, 1964, 1967

HOCKEY HALL OF FAME 1969

•

MRS. ANDRA McLAUGHLIN KELLY

UNITED STATES FIGURE SKATING TEAM—1949-51

Red's heart was shaped like a Red Wings emblem.

—Andra Kelly

I BROKE IN WITH THE DETROIT Red Wings in 1947-48, the year after Gordie made the team.

I was a Red Wing for 13 years and played in 846 games for Detroit.

When Detroit General Manager Jack Adams got rid of me, nobody had ever played as many games as a Red Wing as I had. And I played in 94 playoff games—more than any Red Wing except Ted Lindsay had ever been in.

And, as it happened, I won the Stanley Cup four times as a Red Wing: in 1950, '52, '54, and '55.

What *teams* they were!

We had "Red Wings" painted on our backside, basically! We didn't think there *was* any other team except the Red Wings! We were a group on and off the ice. We were *all* hockey!

Holy Man, you could pass that puck off to quite a few guys who could really do some great wonders. Lindsay and Howe, of course. Gordie and Ted were so close. They stayed together and they played together on the ice. Howe and Lindsay were always looking for one another, because they were together all the time and they'd talk plays, "If I'm here and you're there we do this, and this is how we'll do this," and they'd look for each other. They'd forget sometimes that there was another guy on the line with them. But their center, Sid Abel, was a veteran and he'd tell 'em, "What do you think I am? A statue?"

I never thought I'd play anywhere *but* Detroit. I can still hardly believe I didn't. Here's what happened.

In 1959, late in the season in the spring, I broke my ankle in practice. I got hit by a shot. These things happen. So they put it in a cast, but they don't tell anybody.

Then the team loses two games in a row on the road. And we were struggling that year. It wasn't an easy year, 1958-59. We were struggling, and then they lose three in a row, and they're desperate. We're *all* desperate.

They come to me—Jack and our coach, Sid Abel, and asked, "Could I play?"

The Doctor said it wouldn't do any permanent damage, so he said if I could stand the pain, I could play. So they took the cast off and taped it up. They taped it all the way up way above my knee.

And so I played. *But I couldn't turn.*

First game, I go in against Chicago, and now you've got Bobby Hull coming down against me. You know, *Bobby Hull!* Strong as a bull— fast, hardest shot in hockey. Bobby Hull, Holy Man!

I can't take a chance on him going to my left because that's the direction I can't turn—towards the middle of the ice! I can't turn that way! So I have to play more in the middle and leave a big hole along the boards, so that when he comes, I'm able to turn and go with him. I didn't have a very good night against him, and now it's four losses straight.

Then the game's over and off comes the skate. Then they take the tape off.

You put tape on and take it off your leg all the time. Stuff starts to bleed a little, you know? After a while it starts to get a little tender. That ankle was sore all the way through to the end of the year.

And then we end up missing the playoffs. First time—the only time—Detroit missed the missed the playoffs while I was a Red Wing; the first time Detroit missed the playoffs in *21 years!*

I'd been in the league 11 years, and that was the first time we'd missed out. I played in the League for 20 years, and that was the *only* time my team ever missed out. We finished dead last, in fact. It wasn't an easy year, 1958-59.

I exercised the foot all next summer, using a tennis ball, because Andra told me that Sonia Henie had broken her foot or something, and she used a tennis ball to strengthen it, so I did the same thing.

I figured she knew what she was talking about.

Andra was one of the best figure skaters in the world. Andra was on the U.S. Ladies Figure Skating Team and skated for the United States at the World Championships in 1949, '50 and '51. She finished in the Top 10 twice! Then she skated in ice shows. That's kind of how we met, in fact.

Anyway, Sonia Henie—she won the Ladies Figure Skating gold medal three times at the Winter Olympics, as you know—had told Andra about the tennis ball.

Plus, I ran on the sand beach out in Kingsville, Ontario. I had a cottage out there, and I figured, barefoot in the sand, I'd get my work in.

Now, up at the cottage all summer, all the reports are coming through all the time that my legs are through, you know? Coming out of the Detroit papers, actually!

In Detroit, the press was kind of, mostly, handled by Jack. Whatever he gave 'em, well, they printed it. Not all of them did, but a few of them did.

I'm seeing these reports and I'm thinking, "Well, the brass knows what's happened. What the hang? Why aren't they telling the reporters what happened to me?"

But I really didn't pay any attention to it. The next year, the fall of 1959, I come back and I'm good as new. At Christmas time we're in Toronto here.

Trent Fayne from the *Toronto Globe and Mail*

came up to my hotel room to interview me and he says, "Your team's going better this year and you're playing a little better; how come?"

That gave me a little chuckle, "Well, thanks. I'm glad to hear that. The team's just playing better, that's all."

"Aw, come on," he said. "There's more to it than that. All the reports coming out of Detroit; they say your legs are gone—that you're over the hill."

I thought, "We didn't say anything at the time last spring because we didn't want people taking whacks at my ankle, that's why. If they don't know, they don't take whacks. But now, it doesn't matter. It's over. My ankle isn't broken anymore. So what's the difference?"

So I told Fayne what had happened. I told him the ankle had been broken late the previous season; that they asked me if I could play; that I tried it and that I could get by, but that I couldn't play 100 percent.

So Fayne wrote the story.

Marshall Dan gets it and he puts it in the Detroit paper. It was the *Free Press,* big headline: *Was Red Kelly Forced to Play on Broken Foot?*

I read the story and it didn't say much. The headline, though! I looked and I said, "Holy Man," but then I read the story and it didn't really say what the headline indicated. The story itself didn't play it up nearly as big.

So I thought, "Oh well, no big deal."

Andra Kelly: Then Pat Lindsay called; Ted Lindsay's wife. That was Ted's third and last season in Chicago. He retired at the end of the year. Pat asked, "Andra, are your bags packed?"

"Are our bags packed? What do you mean?" I said.

And Pat said, "Well, Red's going to be going REAL SOON! *Like maybe today!*"

I said, "What? I can't *believe* it!" Red's *heart* was shaped like the Red Wings emblem! He didn't know there *was* any other team besides Detroit!

Red Kelly: We'd only been married six months when this happened, you see, so she didn't know too much about what 13 years with Detroit really meant.

Andra Kelly: Well, we'd been dating for quite some time, and *of course* I knew how he loved that team! I couldn't *believe* that they would do that to him!

Red Kelly: That night, we're playing New York at the Olympia. And they told me—but not until after I'd played the game against the Rangers.

Andra Kelly: It was all through the arena. He's playing the game; it's going all through Olympia. I'm hearing people whispering, this kind of thing.

I was pregnant so my obstetrician was scared something might happen from the shock of it.

So he came down and he said, "Andra, I want to talk to you outside the arena."

"No, I don't want to miss seeing Red play."

But I went out and he whispered, just whispered to me, "Red has been traded."

I said, "No!" The shock *was* great; better hearing it from him.

So I knew.

I had to watch Red play the rest of the night, knowing that he wasn't going to be there anymore.

Red Kelly: After the game was over, they told me to go up and see the General Manager, Jack Adams.

So I went upstairs. I walked up there, and as I'm going down that long corridor along the side of Olympia Stadium, all the way to the front of the building to where the offices are and up the stairs, I hear people say, "You're gone, Kelly!" or whatever.

So I go upstairs, and Jack Adams and Bruce Norris are sitting in the office. Bruce, he's the owner; he's sitting behind his desk.

Now he tells me I'm gone.

Jack tells me he's trading me to New York; me and Billy McNeil for Bill Gadsby and Eddie Shack.

And Adams is calling me—he doesn't call me "Red," now; not anymore.

He's calling me "Kelly."

As in: "Kelly! You're traded to New York."

And all the years I've been "Red! " All the years! I was 13 years in Detroit! I won four Stanley Cups in Detroit!

But now, I'm "Kelly."

So I said, "Well, I'll think about it."

Adams says, "Think? Think! You be there at 8:30 tomorrow morning to meet Muzz Patrick at the Detroit Leland Hotel! What do you mean, *think about it?*"

I said, "I'll think about it."

And out I went.

Andra and I went home and we turned the TV on.

There was our broadcaster, Budd Lynch, doing the sports on TV. He swallowed hard. He had tears in his eyes. And of course as soon as Andra saw Budd break down, well, *she* really broke down.

We thought about it all night. Went to church in the morning; then I just decided I didn't like the way they handled it.

What they said about my legs!

When I'd broken my foot and played!

Playing for them every night!

Doing everything I can to help!

And for them to portray me in the newspapers as being "over the hill!" Do you know how many games I missed in 13 years in Detroit? Twenty-four.

I played any position. I lost a first All-Star team berth one year because they put me up on the forward line for about 20 games and then the writers didn't know how to vote for me—forward or defenseman. I'd been six straight first All-Stars! That would have been seven! That cost me.

But, who cares? It was for *the team*! You know? *That's* who we're playing for! And then they do this? So I said, "Ha, ha! Who needs you?"

First thing Monday morning, I went to work at Renew Tools. I'd worked for them the year before in the summertime as a representative. We re-salvaged tools for the automobile industry. So I was calling on GM, Chevrolet—and everybody's talking about the dang hockey. I can't get away from it!

Then, a few days later, they called us.

Clarence Campbell, the President of the National Hockey League, called me at my home and told me that they would blacklist me:

"You'll *never* be able to play hockey again; you'll *never* be able to referee; you'll *never* be able to coach. You'll *never* be able to be a *stick boy*! You'll be right out of the hockey! And you'll be out forever!"

Campbell told me he was going to try holding Adams off. He said Jack wanted to suspend me, but Campbell said he was going to hold him off, that he wanted to give me time to think about this.

But, "If he suspends you," he says, "you'll be blacklisted from hockey."

I listened to what he said and everything, and I said, "Well, that's fine, Mr. Campbell. Thank you very much for your offer."

But I said, "I've given everything I have to hockey since I've been knee-high to a grasshopper. If that's what you want to do, you go ahead and do it, *because I'm not reporting to New York!* I thought about it."

Just about 10 days go by and King Clancy, Toronto's assistant general manager, called Andra and said, "Would you mind if we flew Red up here and talked to him?"

Andra Kelly: Red came home from work that night and I said, "They want to talk to you in Toronto."

And he said, "Oh, I'll just go and talk to them. I'll be back tonight."

I had his bags packed. I thought, "You're not going to come back tonight! You're going to be there!" So I packed that bag of his so tight!

Red Kelly: A little bag. We didn't want them to think that I'd stay, anyway. I flew under an assumed name out of Windsor. I wore a Hamburg hat, a bumbershoot, and a long turtleneck. At the airport, King Clancy didn't recognize me. I come off in the midst of a bunch of people and Clancy's at the big window there at the old airport and he's looking out. So I walked in around his back and tapped him on the shoulder. He was still looking out the window! He jumped a little, "Whoa! he said, I thought you didn't come!"

We went down and checked me in under an assumed name at the Westbury Hotel, right there by Maple Leaf Gardens. We met, talked. We didn't come to a decision. It was time to go for dinner. We went to Winston's, which was a great big open room with dozens of tables. Here are all the Montreal Canadiens! There's Rocket Richard! He says, "What are you doing here, Red?"

So, we couldn't talk about anything there.

We come back to the hotel and Punch said, "What do you think about playing center against Jean Beliveau?" That's where we're going to start you. If we're going to win the Stanley Cup, we have to go through Montreal. I think you're the last piece of the puzzle to enable us to do that."

About midnight I agreed to come. They want to know if I can start *that night* against Montreal! So they flew my skates in and I dressed.

And I played for seven more years, and we won four more Stanley Cups.

Andra Kelly: Right after Red called to tell me we were going to Toronto; King Clancy called me from the Maple Leafs and said, "What can we do for you, honey?"

I was amazed. I said, "What can you do *for me?*"

"Yeah," he said. "We want to do something special for you, because Red has agreed to play for us here in Toronto. Now, what can we do for *you?*"

"Put No. 4 on his back! I'm used to looking at No. 4!" I said.

"Done!" he said.

I figured it was a lucky number: four Cups for Detroit; No. 4 was wearing 'em, and No. 4 might mean four for Toronto! *And he won them!*

Red Kelly: Anyway, that's how it worked out.

Andra Kelly: We were married on the *4th of July.* And we've got *four kids.* I figured *four* had been a good number for us.

Red Kelly: Four has been a good number, yeah.

Of those four Cups we won in Toronto, we took three straight: 1962, 1963 and 1964. And we beat Detroit in the Final both in 1963 and 1964. Beat 'em in five in '63, then came back from three games-to-two down to beat 'em in seven in 1964.

Playing for Toronto against Detroit, as far as I'm concerned, it was past history. It was gone.

They can go jump in the lake. When they did that, they cut all ties to me, as far as I was concerned. I'm gone, and I'm going for the next team now, and we're going to do whatever we have to do to win!

No way were we going to get beat by Detroit in a playoff if I had anything to say about it! If I had to go through a brick wall, I'd go through that brick wall after what Adams did.

There was no way Detroit was ever going to beat us! *No way!* Not because of the Detroit guys, but because of what management did and how they did it.

When a player's traded, I hear him saying that it doesn't mean anything, that it doesn't affect him. That wasn't the way it was with me, I'll tell you!

When we beat Detroit for the Cup in '64, it meant I had won seven Stanley Cups in my career, more than any other player at that time.

My dad, who just happened to have been a classmate of Jack Adams when they were both at St. Mike's in Toronto, come down to the Olympia from Simcoe, Ontario, when Toronto played here to watch me.

After the first period, he'd stand in the aisle. Now here comes Adams and Norris, and my Dad says to them, "Isn't it funny how the Stanley Cup just seems to follow that boy around?"

From then on, Norris and Adams would get out of their seats, go two or three steps, see my

Dad, and they'd turn around and go the other way!

I won eight Stanley Cups in my career, more than any player who ever played for Montreal. Guys who played all their career with the Canadiens—like Henri Richard, Jean Beliveau and a couple of the others, they would have more. But somebody who played all their hockey *outside* of Montreal, nobody has won more than eight. I won eight.

I got that No. 4 that turned out so lucky for us my second season in Detroit.

In my rookie season, 1947-48, I wore No. 20. I was the fifth defenseman and you were used sparingly—we didn't play on a regular basis. You were used, in and out, in and out. Whenever an important face-off came or something, off you'd go, and they'd send out the veterans.

Just before Christmas, Doug McCaig broke his leg. Big Doug fell in the corner. Nobody near him, but he hit a crack in the ice and just the way he fell, turning, he broke his leg.

So now *I'm* the fourth defenseman. Now, *I* get a lot of play. They see I can do the job, so they trade Doug to Chicago.

He's not too happy about that, I don't think; and he's not too happy *with me*, I think. All I could think was that I was doing what you're supposed to do. You're just doing your job.

The next season, McCaig got me in Chicago. The puck was shot around the net and it was up along the boards on the left side. He was playing defense and I was rushing for it. I knew he was coming, and I tried to get out of the way, but *he nailed me!* Knocked my wind out and I'm crawling around on the ice, trying to pick up my stick.

McCaig was not the only veteran who came after me. *Certainly* as a rookie you were tested. Veterans would try to threaten you. They did everything they could to intimidate you.

If they could, they'd make you slow down a little, or maybe you'd miss a step or something, just because of the *threat* of them going to nail you or hit you, or whatever they did. But once you went around the league a couple times and you held your own, eventually they'd leave you alone.

Before that, though, that's why you got into a few fights. Certainly early in the career, you did. Fernie Flaman in Boston, Big Butch Bouchard up in Montreal; they were just some of the guys I fought.

I was the welterweight champion at St. Mikes in Toronto when I played my Junior hockey there. We had a boxing tournament every year to raise money for the missions. So I could handle myself.

But I was taught by Joe Primeau, my coach at St. Mike's, winning the game was the most important thing. That's when you got the last laugh. And you don't win games in the penalty box. You stay on the ice. That's why, in 20 seasons, I only had more than 30 penalty minutes in a season twice. The most minutes I ever took in an entire season was 39. You don't win games in the penalty box. That's a reason I won the Lady Byng Trophy for "Most Gentlemanly Player" four times.

But boy, some of the fights I saw!

John Mariucci and Black Jack Stewart had a big battle down in Chicago, toe-to-toe. Each one took their best shot. First Mariucci would hit Stewart, and then Stewart would nail him. They didn't really defend too well, but they took the blows and gave them back! Yes, that was a big brawl in Chicago. They were two tough guys.

And Black Jack Stewart was so strong. He was one of the strongest guys I ever knew in the game. His stick was so heavy I could hardly lift it! It was tough to get it off the ice.

He played under all sorts of conditions. There were times Black Jack couldn't even lace up his skates, his back was so bad. But he was still out there playing. And he never said a word about it, either.

Mariucci wasn't the only guy Stewart had it in for, either. Black Jack never liked Teeder Kennedy of Toronto, on or off the ice. They battled.

I was a rookie and we were playing in Toronto. I was coming around the net and Teeder Kennedy came to check me. I made a little move and slipped the puck between his feet and picked it up on the other side.

Kennedy's looking down trying to find the puck, so Black Jack, he really gave Teeder the gear. Then he *laughed* at him. He shouted, "How'd you like that, Teeder?"

I played some with Leo Reise—Radar—but early in my career I played most of the time with Bill Quackenbush. We played on defense together and we roomed together.

Bill used to say on the ice, "Go get him! You've got the young legs, Red. You go get him!"

I was very lucky to come up with and to be a teammate of two All-Stars, Bill Quackenbush and Black Jack Stewart. Leo Reise and Doug McCaig were there at the time when I first came up. They were the four defensemen and I was the fifth.

I was fortunate to play with All-Stars like that and to learn from them. I learned a lot from playing with them, and listening and talking; going over the plays, the mistakes we made, or things that we had to do if we were playing Montreal the next night, or Toronto or whatever.

And you'd hear the stories of the old days. It was just great.

They gave me No. 20 that first year, but the next year I came to camp and the trainer comes out and pulls out a sweater with No. 4 on it.

"This is your sweater," he says.

What he was showing me was that I made one of the four—one of the top four defenseman on the team.

The other guys, the guys on the other teams, they were enemies. Some of teams you hated more than others, I guess, but you didn't want to be friends with *any* of them. You didn't want to see them in the summertime or any time. They were the enemy!

Never more than in the playoffs! We had some battles.

1950? We'd never beaten Toronto. We came in second place our first year in Detroit, 1947-48. We came in first the second year I was there, and both those years we met Toronto in the Finals.

The first year, 1948, Toronto beat us four straight.

The next year, 1949, the same thing happened. Toronto beat us four straight. Two years in a row.

Now, 1950, this is the third year, but this time we're meeting them in the first round.

The very first game, at the Olympia, Gordie gets hurt trying to take out Teeder Kennedy. Gordie comes up along the boards—he was catching Kennedy from behind. Kennedy was a strong skater, but not the fastest skater. Gordie was overtaking him. Just as Gordie got to him, he went to take him into the boards. Well, a lot of people never realized it, but Jack Stewart—remember, he didn't like Kennedy very well.

Jack saw *this* as a pretty good opportunity. Here are the boards, here's Kennedy coming up alongside the boards, and here's Howe. Gordie's got him pinned in between 'em, and there's no place for Kennedy to go, really. Big Jack came in, and he was really going to give it to him!

But it all happened at the same time. Gordie cut in, his stick broke because Kennedy jumped back, and as he jumped back, Kennedy brought his stick up in a reflex move.

The stick broke, Gordie got his eyeball scratched and crashed his head into the boards and fractured his skull. Gordie was on the operating table until 4:30 in the morning or something. They were afraid Gordie might die! They had to drill a hole in his head and drain the blood out and the whole deal, and they didn't know if he'd ever play again, let alone that year.

We had the next game at home, and emotions were running pretty high, you might say.

We had a big free-for-all against Toronto, where everybody was fighting, I remember. It happened when Ted Lindsay was carrying the puck going in their end toward the Toronto net.

Gus Mortson reached out and caught him with his hand under the chin. Not with a punch; he just reached out and, of course, Ted's feet went out from under him, and down he went.

Well, everybody in the rink saw it except the referee. They didn't see it, so the play went on!

And the puck went on around the net and came out on the other side, and then Leo Fogolin took a run at somebody on Toronto and nailed him; and right away they blew the whistle and they gave *him* the penalty.

And so *everything's* going now. They threw chairs on the ice and the fans were on the ice.

Everybody got on the ice and fought. Even the two goaltenders met: Turk Broda of Toronto and our "Apple Cheeks" Harry Lumley. They hated each other! And they tangled at center ice. They were wrapped up in each other's arms and rolling around on the ice, and with all the equipment that they were wearing, neither could get free to land a punch.

So Broda bit him! Lumley just went livid! Broda bit him on the cheek!

Leo Reise got speared by Teeder Kennedy; jabbed like a pitchfork in the face there. Leo came around with his stick and just missed Jim Thompson's head. But he hit him on the shoulder and Thompson went down, and anyway—*everybody* was fighting!

I had the fight with Lynn. I wound up squared off against Vic Lynn.

We won the game that night, 3-1, to even the series, and we beat Toronto in overtime in Game 7, 1-0. Leo Reise scored the goal—his second overtime goal of the series. He was only the sec-

ond guy ever—the only guy other than Mel "Sudden Death" Hill of the Bruins, in fact—to score more than one overtime goal in the same playoff series.

We played the Rangers in the Final. It was the first time they'd been in the Final since they won the Stanley Cup in 1940. In fact, New York hadn't won a single playoff series since they won the Cup.

So wouldn't you know it, they upset Montreal in the first round. So they get to play us for the Cup.

They almost *upset us*, too!

We finished first and New York finished fourth in the regular season. The schedule went from 60 to 70 games in '49-'50 and we had 88 points—the most in NHL history. New York had 67.

New York had a long losing streak—seven games—right near the end of the season. The last loss in the streak came at the Olympia on the next-to-last night of the season. We beat 'em, 8-7. I was thinking of that game when we were getting ready for the Rangers in playoffs. And I was thinking about how we'd only won half the games we played against New York that season.

In 1950, in the playoffs, the Rangers got thrown out of their rink. New York couldn't play their home games at Madison Square Garden, so they played them in Toronto. Two of the games, Game 2 and Game 3, were played in Toronto, and that's as close as the Rangers got to a home game. The other five games were at the Detroit Olympia.

Don Raleigh—they used to call him "Bones," Edgar Laprade, and "Mighty Mouse" Tony Leswick were the Rangers' best players. And they had Chuck Raynor in goal. He used to come out of the net. They used to say Jacques Plante was the first goalie to wander around, but big Raynor used to come out of the net and into the corner and handle the puck, too. He was quite agile on his skates.

They had us on the ropes, actually.

We won the first game in Detroit then we split the next two in Toronto. Those were New York's "home" games. The rest of the games were at Olympia and we led the best-of-seven series, two games to one, so we felt pretty good about things before "Bones" Raleigh beat us with overtime goals in Games 4 and 5. Right there at the Olympia. We come home from Toronto up two games to one; now we're down three games to two.

They used to take us out of town to Toledo during the playoffs, and we'd stay at the Secor Hotel. We had a little gathering after we lost Game 5. Not a meeting, just a little gathering. Black Jack Stewart, who never said too much— he was very quiet—got up. He was a great team guy and very strong. His roommate was Sid Abel. Black Jack got up and he gave everybody a bit of a go, but especially Sid.

Black Jack told Sid that if he didn't knock "Bones" Raleigh around, he'd do it himself. And Stewart said that if he had to do that, he'd hit Sid, too! Sid said he slept all night with one eye open, because Jack was his roommate and he was afraid Stewart *really would* unload on him.

Jack was so uptight that right after his speech he left, and the coat he grabs—he just grabbed the first one off the rack and thought it was his—turns out to be Jimmy McFadden's. Jimmy was a lot shorter than Jack, and Jack's trying to get this coat on. He's up in the air anyway, and now he's struggling, really struggling, to get the coat on. Nobody in the room made a sound— we were all too afraid to—but we had a lot of laughs about that afterwards.

Pete Babando winds up winning the Cup for us with a double overtime goal at Olympia in Game 7. I remember that goal going in. I can still see it. It was the first time a Game 7 in a Cup Final had gone into overtime, much less double overtime. Pretty dramatic!

That was Pete Babando's last game in Detroit. He spent just the one year with us. And that was Black Jack Stewart's last game in Detroit. He'd broken in with Detroit in 1938 and put his name on the Cup twice as a Red Wing.

And that was Harry Lumley's last game in Detroit, too. He'd just won the 1950 Stanley Cup with three shutouts in playoffs and a goals-against of 1.85! And "Apple Cheeks" was only 23!

In July, Jack Adams shipped all three of them off to Chicago.

The 1951-52 Stanley Cup-winning Red Wings. (Courtesy of Robert L. Wimmer)

Can you imagine? The guy who scores the Cup-winning goal, the toughest guy in the league, and the Cup-winning goalie, all three traded less than three months after we'd won that Stanley Cup!

We got quality players in return for those guys, though.

We got Bob Goldham, Metro Prystai, Gaye Stewart, and "Sugar Jim" Henry, the goaltender.

Terry Sawchuk was 20 when he broke in with us in 1950-51 to replace Lumley in goal. He played every game. And he played every game the next year, too. Ukie was a loner a bit, you know. Sometimes he was downright surly. He crouched and he was on his feet. He'd get down-up quick! He didn't give you much. He didn't give you much to see when you were shooting on him.

Nobody wore a mask. It's the way it was in those days. I saw guys get hit. They used to shoot high

at the guys. Lefty Wilson, *our trainer*, went in one night for Toronto at Olympia in 1956. We were playing them, and as it happened Harry Lumley got hurt in the third period. There were still 13 minutes or so left in the game and Lefty was the spare goaltender—the only one in the building that would play for either team in case either goalie got hurt. If the goaltender got hurt Lefty went in.

So Gordie and Ted, their first shots went right past his ear! On purpose, of course! You have to keep 'em loose. You have to keep him on his toes.

Lefty, he was pretty nervous. He was hollering out there. *He didn't give up a goal.* He stoned 'em. *He stoned us!* You had to give him credit because he was nervous as all get-out and those first shots were up in his ears but he didn't give up a single goal to us.

Terry didn't give up a single goal at Olympia in the 1952 playoffs. I can remember winning the

Cup in 1952, yeah. That was the year we won the eight straight and Ukie never got scored on in Detroit.

We opened in Montreal when actually we should have opened up in Detroit. We had home ice, but the Olympia was being used for something, so we lost our home-ice advantage and opened the Final at the Forum.

I was hurt for the whole series, but nobody knew about it.

In the last game of the first round against Toronto they moved me up to center the Production Line between Ted and Gordie because Abel got hurt.

So I moved up and played center between them and it was a close game. We wound up winning 3-1 to take the Leafs in four straight, but at the time—and it was near the end—it was only a one-goal lead for Detroit, I think; one-nothing or 2-1.

I went racing into the corner in the Toronto end to get the puck. I knew Gordie was coming on the right and I was going to pull the puck back to him and he'd have a great chance. But, Jimmy Thomson nailed me. When my hand hit the boards, it broke the bone and I passed out, sort of. Red Story was the referee and I could hear him sort of in a fog, he had hold of me and I could just faintly hear, just like out of a big fog a voice was coming. "Are you alright, Red?"

So, against Montreal in the '52 Final they patched it up by putting a plate over it with

some sponge padding and then wrapping it around my hand with tape. They didn't tell anybody it was broke, of course.

They dressed me, but Tommy Ivan, the coach, didn't use me. I was just sitting on the bench.

Until we got two men short, that is. Then he put me out to be one of the defensemen to kill the two-men short!

I could *get* the puck but I couldn't shoot it out because I couldn't put the pressure on the low hand on the stick—the hand that was broken. I'd get the puck and only way I could move it was by kicking it; leveraging it by kicking the blade of my stick. Which I did. I could check; I could hold check, but that was about all. We got through the two-men short and we killed it and then he didn't use me anymore.

We only gave up two goals to the Canadiens in that Final. Ukie had a goals-against 0.50!

We were proud of that, sure. You were always conscious of that. That's the way we played in Detroit! If we scored three goals, we were going to win 90 something percent of our games. 99 percent, probably, 'cause we didn't give up goals.

We used to go back on the train and I'd sit with the old guys and they'd talk and they'd say, "You know, actually when you get down to it, Ukie only has to make four or five saves a night." I haven't been there too long so I'm kind of, "What? How can that be?"

They'd say, "Well, we steer 'em off. He just has to play the angle. Unless he opens his legs and it goes through, if he just stands there they can't score because of the angle. *They can't score.* If we can keep them far enough out, then he's going to stop them."

But four or five times a night a guy *would get loose* and that's the four or five saves Ukie would have to make. You think, "They're right." But I never thought about it until they said that.

Adams traded Ukie to Boston and then got rid of a lot of players. A lot of players.

Like Marty Pavelich. Oh, Adams let Marty go. He didn't give him a *chance.* After 10 years! He played *10 years* and Jack just said, "That's it." Adams was going to send him to the minors.

Marty asked, "Can I come to training camp?" Because he figured he could beat *somebody* and make the team.

But, no way! The wool was just *cut and dried.* That's it.

Jack was very stubborn. But, he'd go too far! He'd go through the wall; a cement wall!

Adams would come in, pounce on one guy, game after game: Benny Woit. He always had some reason to yell at Benny. And he'd come in and stand right over him. One time, Benny grabbed a handful of oranges and was sitting there eating them and throwing the peels on the floor. Jack slipped on the orange peels and forgot what he was yelling about. He just went off to the back room, yelling at the trainers about the room being dirty.

But, like I said, Jack traded Sawchuk and brought Hall in and Hall played well. He was an All-Star both years he was in Detroit!

And then Jack Adams got mad at Glen Hall the same way.

It still makes me chuckle. Because Glen said something to him—BOOM! He's gone! Hall told Jack to —— off. Something happened on the ice, and Adams came into the dressing room after. He was sitting right near the door, Glen was, and Adams came in right on top of him. Glen said, "—— off!" or something. That was it. He was gone.

He was traded and they had to get Sawchuk back. And so they traded Johnny Bucyk—23 years he played, and Vic Stasiuk. The whole "Uke" Line in Boston he traded to the Bruins except for Bronco Horvath.

There were just a lot of things there. He made the trades. None of them turned out.

Say if we'd had the Uke Line—Bucyk and Stasiuk, anyway—maybe we wouldn't have been struggling so hard that next year when we were getting into the trouble; when things weren't going so good.

When Metro Prystai went to Chicago early in the 1954 season, we almost struck right then and there. Matter of fact, I wasn't going to play!

They decided to bolster Chicago up and send a player from each team to the Blackhawks and Metro was the one they took from us. They broke us up! We figured they were trying to deplete our team so we wouldn't win again because, at the time, we'd won five regular season championships in a row!

Right before the game the crowd was in the stands and we weren't going out. But they finally, you know, put the act on that the people were in the stands and they went through the whole deal, but we came very close, *very close*, to not going out on that ice.

It was—it was not a very good thing, what they did. That was one of the beginning things, in fact.

Two years later, that union was getting underway and a few teams shipped a few guys out. Toronto shipped Tod Sloan and Jimmy Thomson to Chicago. Seems strange, doesn't it? Thomson was the Leafs captain but it didn't matter. It was done because of that union thing, or at least that's what we all thought at the time.

So, since Lindsay was the guy who started the Association, Jack, he got down on Ted. I never saw him come in and say things to Ted in the dressing room but you knew he was down on him.

Andra Kelly: Jack Adams was instrumental in our meeting, actually. That's right. We met in Carl's Chophouse. I was skating with the ice show and the manager of the ice show, Tommy King, knew Adams. They suggested that we should get together, Red and me. Both redheads, both Irish, McLaughlin and Kelly? That looks good.

That was one side of it. The other side was getting Red to come to the restaurant.

Red Kelly: I didn't want to go. I came because of Gordie. He was going to meet Barbara Ann Scott, the figure-skating star. They were going to introduce them because they'd written in the newspaper that Gordie and Barbara Ann were going together and were going to be engaged. Gordie had never even met Barbara Ann Scott in person! And supposedly they were engaged!

Many years later King tells me, "You know how that story got started?" I was the publicity guy for the Chicago Stadium. I started that to sell tickets in Detroit!"

Gordie wanted somebody to accompany him. Ted didn't want to do it and I didn't want to do it either. Then I thought, "Okay, I'll go with you, Gordie. I'll keep you company."

After all of this, Barbara Ann Scott wasn't even there! But Andra and her mother and brother were there. And they said, "Would you like to meet another star, Andra McGlothlin?"

"Oh, yeah," I said. So we met her and her family.

Andra Kelly: That was the start!

Red Kelly: That was over 50 years ago; 1952! We were married in '59. Jack gave Andra away at our wedding. Then, six months later, he gave me away!

But, it worked out.

TED LINDSAY

DETROIT RED WINGS 1944-1957, 1964-65

CHICAGO BLACKHAWKS 1957-1960

HEAD COACH DETROIT RED WINGS 1979-1980

GENERAL MANAGER DETROIT RED WINGS 1977-1980

STANLEY CUP 1950, 1952, 1954, 1955

HOCKEY HALL OF FAME 1966

I HATED EVERYBODY I played against, and they hated me.

It was a wonderful way to play hockey. It was the only way to play hockey!

I had a gift from the good Lord, and it was that I hated to lose. He made sure I had a competitive spirit.

There was only one reason I dressed in the uniform. Sure, I loved the game—there was no doubt about that—but when we started the game, there was only one reason we were there. And that was to win!

I wasn't there to entertain anybody sitting in the seats. They talk about sports today. It's all showmanship; it's *entertainment*. I never looked at myself as an entertainer. I looked at myself as a skilled craftsman; a carpenter, something like that. A skilled hockey player, that's what I was.

It was all self-done. We were all self-motivated. *You knew your game.* And the guys were pros. All of our guys were. And all the guys you played against were. I played with and against the greatest hockey players who ever played. A lot of people don't know their names, but they were the greatest hockey players who ever played the game. Even with the talent that you have today.

I always believed *everything* is intimidation. You intimidate people in many different ways. You study people.

OPPOSITE: Ted Lindsay shows his excitement by kissing the Stanley Cup. (Courtesy of Robert L. Wimmer)

We played each other 14 times a year, every year. Take the Canadiens. Montreal would come to Olympia Stadium seven times. We'd go to The Forum seven times. Every year. Same with all the other teams. We'd play them 14 times—seven at Olympia and seven on the road. So you got to know people. You knew who the tough ones were.

You knew who wasn't tough. All you'd have to do is say "boo" to scare some of 'em off. More than you'd think, too. This might seem odd for a lot of hockey fans, that you could scare guys just by saying "boo," because fans think everybody who plays hockey has a lot of guts. But there are a lot of guys who play hockey who don't have a lot of guts.

I did a lot of talking on the ice, all the time. Because I was into the game! But I had to be into it. I had to be either causing trouble or trying to get out of trouble. It all goes back to intimidation. You can intimidate by words or you can intimidate by physical force.

I had a *very* foul mouth when I was playing. I *never spoke* on the ice unless it was an expletive. *Everybody* was an S.O.B.

We used to insult the Frenchmen. We had, of course, Marcel Pronovost and Marcel Bonin on our team, and one night I'm skating past the Montreal bench and big Butch Bouchard says, "But, Teddy! You have the Frenchmen *on your team*." So I said, "Yeah, but we have *the smart ones*."

I practiced the way I played. There's no differ-ence. And it's the same when you're talking about Gordie Howe. *Any guy* that played against Gordie on the left wing, they had a tough time at training camp.

Howe was fighting for his job. It wasn't assured. Our two farm teams, Edmonton in the Western League and Indianapolis in the American League—hell, we had guys there who were as good as we were! That was their weapon over us. No, we were there to earn a job—every one of us, every year.

That was another thing from our time. *You fought your own battles.* They didn't have policemen; they didn't have the enforcers and all that. You got yourself in trouble, you got yourself out.

I ran into an awful lot of good men in my life—and I'm talking about fighting. Guys that were tough, guys that were strong. I got my ears pinned back lots, and I guess I pinned back a few, too.

You never had to get a guy back that night or the next shift. We played each other so often, so you had rivalries. You *knew* you were going to get him again.

So, if you're any kind of competitor—and he knew what kind of a competitor you were, and he got you dirty—he *knew* he was going to get it back. He didn't know when, though! That was the beauty of it.

OPPOSITE: From left: Gordie Howe, Red Kelly, Jimmy Skinner, and Ted Lindsay. (Courtesy of Robert L. Wimmer)

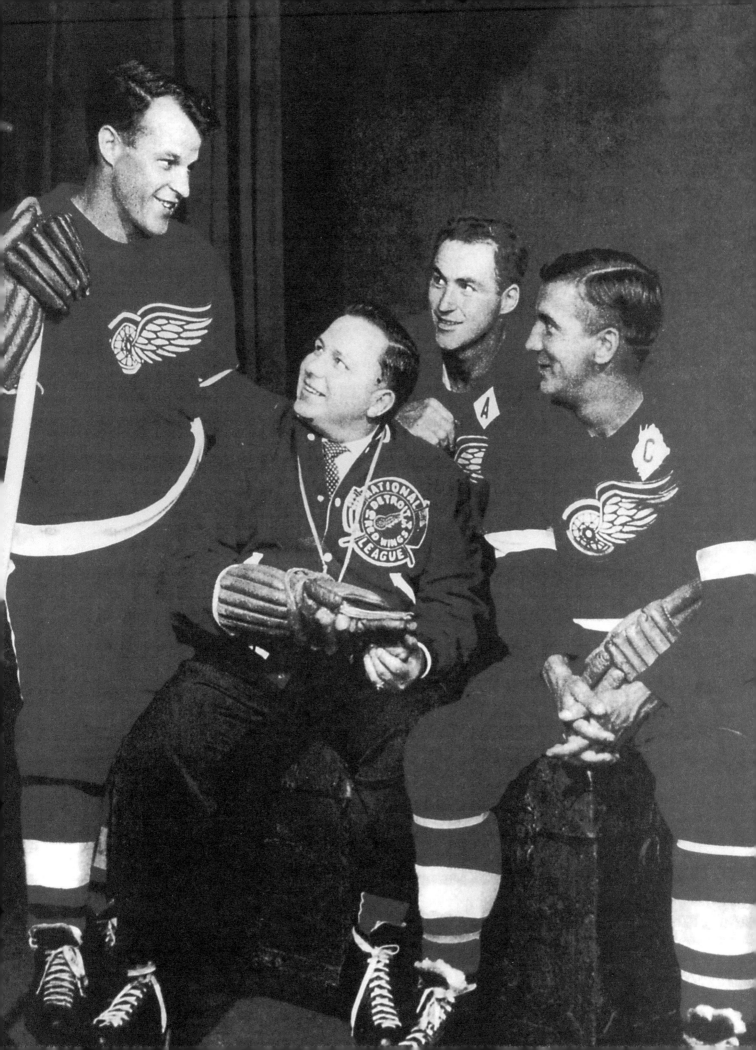

Playing so often, you'd maybe have a chance to get him some time, but you'd let it go and he'd think, "Gee, he didn't give it to me that time. He must have forgotten."

But eventually he'd learn that you hadn't!

You'd simply wait for the right time. There's no rush to get it done. And we try to do it—not that we were sneaky people or anything—but we try to do it when the referee doesn't see us. No sense getting a penalty. Besides, we get enough stupid ones without getting nailed for some we might actually have deserved.

I learned early. We were playing one night in Montreal in my rookie season, 1944, and Elmer Lach comes up to me and says, "You're having a pretty good night there, kid." He was older so he was calling me kid. So I'm skating and I'm thinking, "He's not a bad guy. He made a statement like that, he can't be such a bad guy, right?"

The next shift, I get the lumber laid on me by him. All he did was, he took my guard down. So it was another lesson, and a good lesson. He was smart and I was dumb.

Even before the National Hockey League, I learned. I went to St. Mike's in Toronto to play Junior in 1943. Bill Ezinicki, who was probably 15 pounds heavier than me, and at least a couple of inches taller than me, was playing for Oshawa Generals. They were the powerhouse of junior hockey in Canada. Ezinicki had already been playing a couple of years for Oshawa when I got to St. Mike's. Everybody said, "He's tough and he's going to intimidate you."

My attitude to myself was, "He bleeds the same as I do, and if anybody is going to think he's going to chase me out of the rink, he's crazy! Because I'll take what he gives, and I'll give what I can give."

We both made it to the National Hockey League the next year, 1944. "Wild Bill" was with the Leafs, and I was with the Red Wings, of course.

We had a number of run-ins, as you might imagine, but they always talk about that fight I had with Ezinicki in '51 after Ezzie had been traded to Boston. You always hear them call it a "stick-swinging duel," The thing is, the sticks weren't swung that much. There were two swings of the stick. That's all.

We were playing Boston at Olympia, another sellout for the Red Wings. Ezzie and I ran into each other at the blue line right in front of the Boston bench. He hit me with his stick right over the head at the hairline where the forehead and the hair met, and he parted my skull. Blood started to run and I thought, "If I let him get away with that, my hometown fans are going to think I might be a chicken."

So I took my stick—he was standing there—and I whacked him. When I whacked him, he dropped his stick and his gloves. Well, I couldn't hit him with the stick again because now *he* didn't have one.

So I dropped my stick and we started with the fists. It was a good night for me. I don't know where his mind was, or maybe he wasn't as good a fighter as I thought, but he was a good fighter and he was strong. I just happened to have everything going for me. I caught him and happened to knock a couple of teeth out and cut him over the eye for a few stitches.

George Gravel was the referee I remember, and George says, "You're through for the night for using the stick!"

So I thought, "Good! I'm out of here and I'm not in too bad of shape." I've got only the one cut where Ezinicki hit me with his stick.

I'm going down along the boards toward our bench to get off the ice and Gordie Howe yells out, "Look out! Here he comes!"

I turned around and Ezinicki had broken away from the linesman. He was coming at me like a raging bull. I swung and I hit him right under the jaw. It lifted him up and he came down on the seat of his pants, and he hit his head on the ice. As soon as he went down, I straddled him and I grabbed his sweater with one hand and pulled while I punched with the other.

Gordie yells, "Hey Ted, he's out! He's unconscious!"

I said, "I don't give a damn. I want to kill him!"

Then I recognized that he *really was* hurt. I didn't think that he was at the start. I only wanted to make sure he didn't get up. That's what I wanted.

So I went in the dressing room and I showered and then I went to the first aid room which was down a hall from our dressing room. The way

we played the game, we hated each other, but we also respected each other. You all respected each other. So I opened the door and I said, "Are you all right, Ezzie?"

He wasn't too happy to see me. He screamed, "I'll get you, you S.O.B!"

We were suspended for the balance of the season for games involving our clubs. I couldn't play in Boston and he couldn't play in Detroit. They figured, by the next year, some of this stuff might have died down. I forget what the fine was, but it was the biggest the league had handed out in 18 years. It was a lot of money. You know, when you're making $5,500 a year, $300 is quite a chunk.

I'll tell you another guy who was tough. John Mariucci. And he was a good hockey player besides. He was an All-American football player, and he was also an All- American hockey player at the University of Minnesota. He played for the Blackhawks in my first years. Mariucci was tough as nails. They didn't make them any tougher.

The only guy tougher than him was Black Jack Stewart. It was funny. Those guys had their own rivalry.

Black Jack was there when I went to my first training camp with Detroit. I remember the excitement of it. It was the fall of 1944. I was 19.

It was very exciting being in the same room with those NHL players. All through training camp,

I practiced with Joe Carveth and Murray Armstrong. Joe Carveth was a smooth skater, just nothing but grace and style. He never got ruffled. He never got excited. And he could play hockey that way. Those two did everything they possibly could to help me. I got through training camp with the help of Joe Carveth and Murray Armstrong. I'll go to my grave thinking they were the finest people I met in hockey.

It was not an easy camp.

There were guys on the team—and I can understand now that I've gotten older—who looked at me as somebody who was going to take their job. I'd just as soon not name those guys. They were there. A lot of it was their personality, and a lot of it was they were threatened. I figured, if you can't keep your job with a young kid trying to take it, then you don't deserve to have the job.

We trained over in Windsor that year. The hottest September I can remember! Windsor Arena back in those days was no better than it is today. There's no air conditioning. It was difficult for them to even keep ice in the place.

It was the tail-end of the war, and there were about four guys on the Red Wings team who were working during the day at the Ford Motor plant on war jobs. And they couldn't get off work. They had to work during the day. And then they came to practice at night, at 6 o'clock.

One day Adams says to me, "You're going to practice with the veterans."

I was thrilled to death. Until I got in there the first night, and I had to put this equipment on that somebody had worn in the morning!

They didn't have drying rooms in the Windsor Arena so *everything* was wet. And *everything* was cold. And *everything* smelled. After a couple of days, I'm thinking, "This is the National Hockey League? I'm better off back at St. Mike's playing junior hockey!"

I could still play another year of junior hockey. I was thinking that if I was going to play junior again, at least I'd play a lot. I thought I'd play 30 or 40 minutes a game for St. Mike's.

I didn't think in my own mind I was going to play with the Red Wings, at least not much. And I wasn't going to sit on the bench or not dress.

When I'm in Windsor a few days, Adams says, "Well, we want you to sign with the Red Wings."

I said, "No, I'm going back to St. Mike's."

After about two weeks of training camp, Adams called Father Mallon at St. Mike's and says "What are you offering this kid Lindsay to play for you this year?"

Father Mallon, the athletic director said, "We're not offering him anything, why?"

Adams says, "Because all I got out of him was, 'I'm going back to St. Mike's,' and I want to know why."

From left: Marty Pavelich, Jack Adams, and Ted Lindsay. (Courtesy of Robert L. Wimmer)

So my coach, Paul McNamara, called me in Detroit after he talked to Father Mallon. Paul knew I wasn't going to become a doctor or lawyer or Indian chief, or something like that. He knew where my heart was.

Paul says, "You know, Ted, opportunity comes once in a lifetime. If you don't take it, you might never get it again."

I took that advice, but I told Mr. Adams, "I want a 'No Minor League' clause in my contract."

We were only playing 50 regular-season games at that time, so I also told him, "And I want to be able to play at least 40 games and not sit on the bench. I want to play."

Mr. Adams put that in writing for me. I got a $2,000 bonus for signing my amateur card away—which was unheard of, astronomical.

And I played in 45 of those 50 games in 1944-45, plus all 14 in the playoffs when we lost out to Toronto in the Final. We were down 3-0 in that series before we won three straight. Then we lost Game 7 in Toronto.

I never *dreamed* of playing in the National Hockey League. I never knew where I was going. I knew I loved hockey, and I took it one game at a time. One day at a time. One year at a time. It just all evolved. I got better and I got better and I got better, and got more competitive, and I got more skills, and it all came together.

Probably, without hockey, I would have been in the mines up in Kirkland Lake, Ontario. That's where my thoughts were when I turned pro.

I got a two-year contract from Detroit, and I thought after the two-year contract, I'd go back to work in the mines for the rest of my life. Two years became three, three years became four and, you know, the rest is history.

I hear people say, "Gee, these guys making this money today."

I look at that and I think about how I came from a place, Kirkland Lake, in the Depression. I was the youngest of nine children.

My dad lost everything in the Depression. So, dad moved up to Kirkland Lake, which at that time had the largest gold mines in the British Empire. The thinking was if there is a Depression, then go where there is gold. They work the mines 24 hours a day, seven days a week.

I always called Kirkland Lake home because that's where my grade school was, my high school was, my hockey was—and so when I think of hockey, I always think of Kirkland Lake. It was a great place to grow up: 15 degrees below zero weather all winter long, for about four months, so most every other or second or third home had a rink in its backyard.

I was nine before I even put a pair of skates on—a pair given to me by a lady down the street, as a matter of fact. Before that, I was nine years of age, *living in Canada*, and I didn't know how to skate. I was a retarded Canadian, I guess. Ha, ha.

My goal was to play hockey and have fun with it, and grow up with it, and develop with it, and that was it. I never envisioned playing in the National Hockey League. That was not my goal.

My dad, Bert, played in the NHL. He was a goaltender in the NHL in 1917; the first year there *was* a National Hockey League. Dad played for the Montreal Wanderers in 1917-18, and for the Toronto Arenas in 1918-19. My dad never talked too much about his game. When my dad played, the goaltenders couldn't drop at all. Not just flop, they couldn't drop. They were not allowed to drop at all to make a save. The rule was that goalies could not leave their skates to make a save, so they had to pretend they were falling. Falling wasn't against the rules.

Former Red Wings trainer Lefty Wilson holds up the familiar #7 jersey of Ted Lindsay after he was traded to Chicago in 1957. From left: Johnny Wilson, Tom McCarthy, Forbes Kennedy, Guyle Fielder were all vying for the position vacated by Lindsay. (Courtesy of Robert L. Wimmer)

When I was growing up, he had his goal pads. He still had those. They didn't give you as much protection as the forwards' shin pads today. They're a little wider, but that's about it.

When I broke into the NHL, my dad became only the second man ever to play in the NHL and have his son play in the NHL. Lester Patrick played *one game* in the NHL in the 1920s, then had two of his sons—Muzz and Lynn—play for him in the 1930s and '40s when he was general

manager of Rangers. If not for Lester Patrick playing in that one game, my dad would have been the first NHL player ever to have a son also play in the league.

But my dad never pushed me; he never pushed me. My dad never even talked too much to me about playing hockey. When I played, when I came home at night after a game, dad—if he was not too tired—he'd sit in the living room with the paper, and if I came in and if I wanted to talk, he'd talk. He had to get up early in the morning to go to work in the mine, but if I wanted to talk to him, he would.

He would never say, "You played a good game," or "You played a bad game," or anything like that. He never would.

One thing I'll say about dad. He was a great father. He wasn't one of these fathers that you have around these rinks nowadays.

Marty Pavelich and I had the first hockey school in North America. We had a hockey school in Port Huron, Michigan, for 18 years. We used to say that if we could just keep the parents out of the rinks, we could let the kids just have fun, learning how to play what I think is the greatest game in the world.

I guess it's like anything. Everybody has pride in their child. They've got their genes, so they *can't* be able to do *anything* wrong. They can only do everything right.

But to some parents, I'd say, observe what your child is doing—trying to learn how to skate on an eighth-of-an-inch of blade, with about two or three inches of it on the ice. It's almost like a trapeze artist; a balancing act.

Just imagine yourself putting the skates on *your* feet and going out there trying to control a little black thing on the ice. Think about *how difficult* that is! Think about how difficult it would be for you, and put it in the context of your son, or daughter, now, as more girls are playing. Olympic gold medals in women's hockey—and that's wonderful, too.

Put yourself in your son's position. He's younger; he doesn't have the strength that you have. So if you think it's going to be difficult for you, or if you think you couldn't even do it, then be very grateful when you see he's able to go from the bench to the face-off position, or to make a rush and get back. Let the kids grow up!

And I had a great mother. My mother never saw me play until I played my first game for the Detroit Red Wings in Maple Leaf Gardens in 1944. Back in those days, mothers were the family—laundry lady, cook, sewer, washer. You didn't have automatic washers, you didn't have automatic dryers; everything had to be hung out on a line. You had to scrub a lot of the things yourself on a scrub board. They were real women back in those days!

But back to the Detroit Red Wings!

I would have liked to have played for Detroit my whole life, but, you know, funnier things have happened. When Adams broke the team up, that was a major thing.

Going back to '55 when we won the Stanley Cup over Montreal when Adams was general manager; when they said we were lucky we won it; when they said we only won it because Rocket Richard had been suspended.

That's where Adams made the biggest, stupidest, dumbest move that anybody ever made in their life in hockey.

That summer, he traded nine players Detroit had away from that championship team. I think he sent four to Chicago and two to Boston, but it might have been three to Boston and two to New York. But when it was over, Detroit had lost seven, nine players. That's half a team!

Two years after that, in February, 1957, we announced the formation of the NHL Players Association. I was the guy who started the Association. In July, 1957—five months later—I'm traded to Chicago.

I was a Red Wing for 14 years. After Sid Abel went to Chicago in 1952, I was captain for four. In those four years, we won the Cup twice and were in the Finals another time. The only season we didn't make the Finals, we won the regular season. I'm proud of that.

So, how did I find out I'd been traded by Detroit—traded by Jack Adams—to Chicago, after I'd been a Red Wing since 1944? How did I find out I was gone after we won eight league championships? After we won four Stanley Cups?

It was in the newspaper. That's how I found out.

We finished first that season. I was 32 and I had my best year ever as a Red Wing:

- More goals and points than when I won the Art Ross Trophy for NHL Leading Scorer in 1950.
- A 30-goal season; my fourth.
- 85 points, which, at the time, was both the fifth-best scoring season in Red Wings history and the most points ever scored in a season by a Red Wing not named Gordie Howe.

So how did I find out I was gone? Like I said, it was in the newspaper. Jack Adams never called me. But Jack *was talking*—to the press. He was telling the press how much money I was making. He lied. He was telling them what a trouble-maker I was. He lied.

I had my best season ever in 1956-57. Gordie and I finished 1-2 in scoring, and I assisted on a few of the 44 goals he got. I was 32.

I was 32. I went to Chicago and I existed for three years. I was treated well there by management even, and I was treated well by the fans. I only had one good year and that was my last year that I played with Ed Litzenberger and Tod Sloan. My first year there was Bobby Hull's first year in the National Hockey League. My second year was Stan Mikita's first year, he was my center man. That was a great thrill.

As for Hall, you know why *he* got traded? Adams told him not to talk to me.

When he played for Windsor Juniors I didn't hang around the bars, so if I had a night out, I'd go over to watch the Spitfires play. After the game was over I'd go up—and it wasn't that I was much older than those guys, probably seven years older, but still from 18 to 25 five is quite a difference—so I'd go up and just visit with them and be on my way. I did this many, many times. I enjoyed young people.

So, I knew Glenn since he was a kid playing junior hockey over in Windsor. When he came to Detroit, Adams told him, "Don't talk to him; he's bad for you," or something.

Glen said, "Mr. Adams, he's never done anything to me. And if I want to talk to him, *I'll talk to him.*"

And that is why he was traded, strictly. And for the next 16 years *after* he was traded to Chicago, he was the best in the National Hockey League. And the Red Wings are looking for a goaltender for all of those years.

We should have won!

We should have won *many more* Stanley Cups than the four we *did win* in the 1950s. Montreal won five Stanley Cups in a row right after that, and to this day, every time I hear about Henri Richard having 11 Stanley Cup rings, I'm happy for him.

But I'm sad because of the fact that five of those Stanley Cup rings he has should have been ours. And maybe six or seven of them.

We had Terry Sawchuk in the net. Greatest goaltender who has ever played, for the first five years of his career. Never will be a better one. I don't care who. And we had Glen Hall playing in Windsor. We had the greatest hockey player of all time—Howe.

We only had one weakness on our team at that time and that was on defense. That was the only weakness on our team, but even then it wasn't going to be a weakness for maybe another two years, and only then because Bob Goldham was getting a little older. Bob was a great team player, unbelievable. Bob died way too young.

Montreal wanted Sawchuk, and Adams didn't want to make the deal because it would make them stronger. Hell, they won the Stanley Cup five years in a row; how much stronger could you make them?

Adams could have gotten possibly Tom Johnson and Doug Harvey. Neither one of them had really established themselves at that time yet.

If we would have got Tom Johnson, *we* would have won the five that Montreal won.

If we would have gotten Harvey, we'd have probably won seven or eight!

People say, "Lindsey's pipe dream." But, no, I really believe it. We had the talent. We had the depth. We had a system.

The nine players he traded in 1955, that was what broke that team up! It *never* should have been broken up!

Jack Adams thought he was Jesus Christ.

I don't mean that as sacrilege. But, names didn't mean a thing. Bodies were what he wanted, and he thought because he was Jack Adams, all he had to do was put a guy in a Red Wing uniform—and he was going to be good *because* Jack Adams put him in a Red Wing uniform. Uh, uh, not true. He destroyed that franchise, he really did.

And up until Steve Yzerman came here in 1983, that franchise floated up and down—and more down than up. And it stayed down until they got Yzerman.

To me, Steve Yzerman is the greatest Red Wing ever.

What I saw in 2002 when Detroit won the Stanley Cup with him, what he has done in his career: He's the greatest Red Wing who's ever played. And that includes Howe. I mean it. Yzerman is a winner. He's proved that.

As I've always said, Gordie Howe is the greatest hockey player who ever played.

But Gordie wasn't a winner. Gordie couldn't make it happen. He could make it happen for

players in the National Hockey League. Marty Pavelich was very intelligent—probably one of the most intelligent hockey minds that was never utilized by coaching or anything like that.

The former general manager of Dallas, Bob Gainey, used Marty as the epitome of what it means to be a two-way forward when he played for Montreal.

For a time, it was my job to stop the Rocket. But then, very quickly after that, because we had the Production Line, Marty Pavelich took over. Marty could put the Rocket to sleep a little

> "As I said before, I'll say it again, that's the way hockey should be played."
>
> —TED LINDSAY

himself, because of his talent. If you look at the record, Gordie played in the Finals 10 times and won three. Remember, he got hurt in the first game of the playoffs in 1950, which we won, but he didn't play.

We had good teams.

But, Jack made many stupid moves. Take 1957. That was one of the stupidest moves he ever made. The season was over and we got beat out by Boston in the first round. This is the summer that Hall and I got traded to Chicago. And where Adams thought Marty Pavelich was finished.

Hell, Marty could have played another five years. He was one of the best defensive hockey

bit because he was a diplomat. He didn't rile him. Marty would say, "He's great enough. I don't want to get him angry and make him greater, so I'll kind of try to subdue him a little bit."

Of course, Marty was with Glenn Skov and Tony Leswick on a line. Because of that line— our checking line—I always figured every game we played, we started half a goal ahead!

In those days, every team had a scoring line and they had a checking line, and all the checking lines went against the best line from the other team. So every night, these guys—Pavelich, Skov and Leswick—played against the best players the other team had. But besides stopping them, these guys, our checking line, they'd each end up with anywhere from eight to 12 goals a year. That was a tremendous advantage for the Detroit Red Wings.

To people today, eight to 12 goals doesn't mean anything. But then, 20 goals was the standard. I always say that 20 goals back then was like hitting .325 in baseball.

I won the Art Ross Trophy in 1949-50. I had a good downshift of speed. I could be coming at you, and I could go inside or I could go outside. If I got you on the outside, I could give a downshift and just accelerate and cut in.

I had an awful lot of goals I used to put up over the goalie's right shoulder. We didn't have the slapshot in those days; we didn't have the curved sticks. But we were accurate. We knew where the puck was going.

And you got to know your goaltenders. Every goaltender has his good spot, and every goaltender has his weak spot. As long as you could get to his weak spot, that's where you went.

But, back to the summer of '57, when Adams told Marty he was all finished. "We are going to send you to the minors," he said.

Well, the thing was, Marty was a smart businessman. And, by then, Marty and I had our own business. We had started in 1952. This is '57. The two of us couldn't make a living out of our business yet, but we were getting there. That was our goal when we were finished with the hockey.

Marty just stared at him. Then he said, "Mr. Adams, I just retired." And he walked out.

The greatest thrill of Marty's life was to be able to do that and not have to bend to Jack Adams. He was so happy about that! It was a shame because you know other teams wanted him. Milt Schmidt, the GM in Boston, wanted him because they knew how good he was. He would have helped them for three years, at least.

Yeah, Marty had a system for playing against Rocket Richard. I played against the Rocket for 15 years.

Rocket Richard hated my guts. He wanted me dead.

I hated his guts and I wanted him dead.

As I said before, I'll say it again, that's the way hockey *should* be played.

After I retired in 1965, I used to go to the Maritimes in the winter to play a charity game to raise money for a college hockey team there. They'd have a lot of Montreal old-timers there, and some Toronto old-timers, and some other old-timers from around the league.

We get into our room and I'd see the Rocket. *He wouldn't acknowledge me.* I'd look over at him and give him the nod. Nothing! It was like I wasn't even in the room!

This went on for a couple, three years. Every time I'd nod, but he refused to recognize me. The fourth or fifth year, I gave him a nod and *he nodded back.*

A team photo for the 1953-54 Stanley Cup-winning Red Wings. (Courtesy of Robert L. Wimmer)

And I figured, "Well, well, the ice is starting to melt."

We didn't become social friends or anything like that, but we did become friends. We would go out of our way to say hello to each other, and I became closer to him.

Before he died, he told me something that I will take to my grave with me.

It was the greatest compliment I've ever had in my life.

If I told somebody this, they'd never believe it, so I wanted to get it on tape. But he was getting so sick, and I didn't want him to think I wanted this on tape before he died, you see? And I never did get the tape done, and I regret that to this day. But it doesn't matter because it mattered only to me anyway.

I will not tell you what he said. I will take it to my grave with me. That's fine. That's where it's going to go. You're delving. You're a typical newsman. I understand that.

I will say this. I always respected the Rocket's talents. There's *no doubt about that.* He was the greatest hockey player who ever played from the blue line in. I've said that a hundred times, at least. Howe was the greatest hockey player, complete player. But from the blue line in, even all these great hockey players they have today, *nobody* played it from blue line in like the Rocket.

They all hated me, but I hated them. But, it all worked out. I formed the Players' Association. The only difficulty there was that we didn't speak to each other. That's an uneasy way to put an organization together—when you don't talk to each other.

in the mail and we'd end up getting about $2,235.

Instead of having 20 playoff shares, Adams was having 28! You should ask Leo Reise about that. Leo was an accountant. He was a numbers man.

"We had a **pretty good thing going** at one time, Gordie and I. Sure, we did. Certainly we were close; we were that. But, **it's happened before** in sports, and I guess it will happen again."

—TED LINDSAY

But, a lot of the guys knew the injustice because everybody joined it except Ted Kennedy from the Maple Leafs. He just kept it to himself. He just kept it to himself. And the guy put $100 in. Ted didn't believe in it, didn't think it was right, I guess. That's his choice. It's a free society.

It didn't surprise me at all that every player in the league signed up except for one. I was surprised that there was one who didn't.

One of the things that got us thinking was our playoff bonus one year after we won the Stanley Cup; 1954 or '55. You never got your playoff check until the middle of the summer. If you won the league championship and won the semifinals, and won the Final, you should have gotten $3,000. One summer, the checks came

But we never could find out where the rest of this money went to. Adams? We didn't know if he was pocketing it, or what. I don't know if Jack was keeping it, and he's not here to defend himself so, whatever. Whoever. Whether it went to the Detroit Hockey Club or what, I don't know.

But, anyway, we didn't get what we wanted. That was major as far as the Red Wings were concerned.

But then, there were other major things. The pension plan. A few things like that. You know, you couldn't even take your own contract out of Jack's office.

So, I decided I was going to do this—start the NHL Players' Association. I hadn't even been

approached by any hockey players, even the Red Wings. Nobody.

I thought about it a year or two before I even talked to Bob Feller about an Association. And I talked to him because I just felt, if I'm going to do it, I want to do it right. Bob was the head of the American League Baseball Players' Association. I wanted to get some direction from him. So I talked to him, and I talked to their lawyers, and we all agreed that if you're going to do it, you don't put it together unless you have the Toronto Maple Leafs and the Montreal Canadiens.

And more so Montreal. So I talked to Doug Harvey from the Canadiens. Doug was very intelligent; he knew all the injustices.

I talked to him before the 1956 All-Star game. That All-Star Game is where we had our first meeting. I wanted to plant the seed, because if you couldn't get Montreal, you couldn't get an Association.

It all would have worked out good if it wasn't for Adams and Gordie.

And look at what happened. Toronto got rid of Jim Thomson. When you talk to some of the Toronto players who played at that time, Teeder Kennedy or someone, they'll tell you. Thomson was on every power play, he was on every penalty-killing play. He never missed one. Now, *that's a valuable hockey player*. Jim Thomson

should be in the Hall of Fame, he really should. I look at the guys who are in there and they don't even have half the talent. Jim Thomson died way too young.

I don't dwell on that subject; The Players Association and all of that. And I don't talk to Gordie anymore.

We had a pretty good thing going at one time, Gordie and I. Sure, we did. Certainly we were close; we *were* that. But, it's happened before in sports, and I guess it will happen again.

I know Colleen, Gordie's wife is not well. I'm sorry to see that, to hear about that. There's no question about that.

But that doesn't change the circumstances. I doubt Gordie and I talking again will ever happen. But who knows what will happen?

I don't dwell on that subject. There are many, many things that are mine and will stay with me, and that are nobody's business. And nobody will know. To the grave, that's where it's going to go.

OPPOSITE: Ted Lindsay speaks into a microphone after receiving the Stanley Cup presented by NHL President Clarence Campbell, left. The Red Wings beat the Montreal Canadiens, 4-3, to win the Stanley Cup finals in 1955. (AP/WWP)

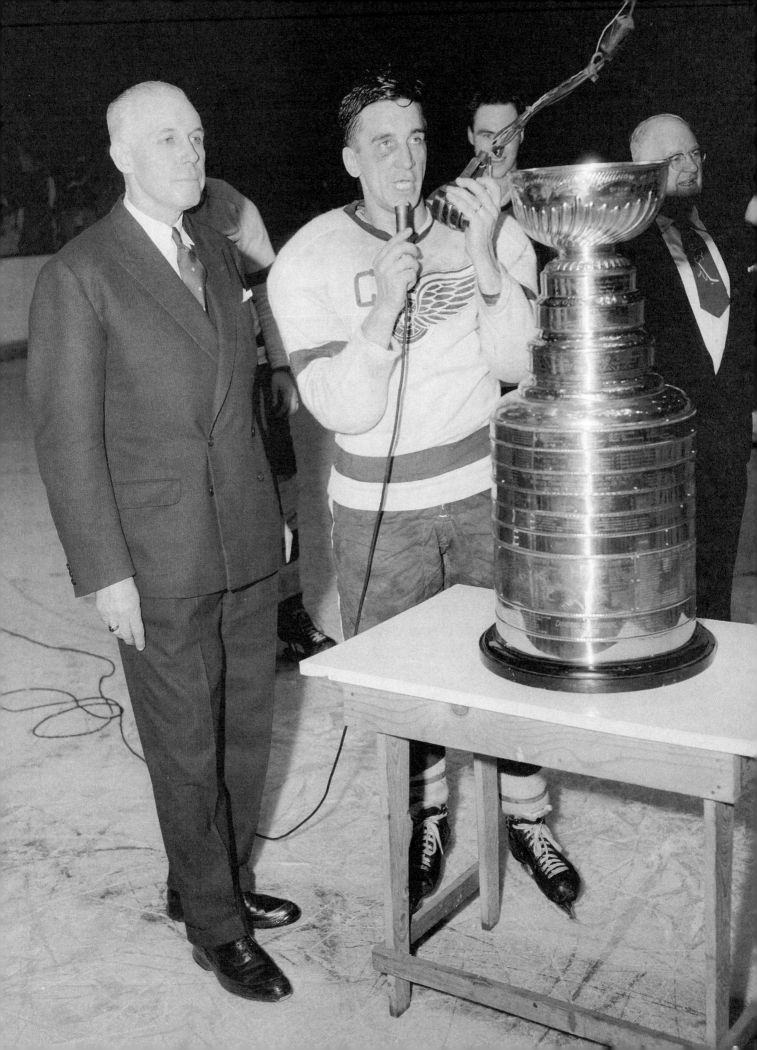

LEO REISE

"Radar"

Chicago Blackhawks 1946

Detroit Red Wings 1946-1952

New York Rangers 1952-1954

Stanley Cup 1950, 1952

THE NEW YORK RANGERS TRIED to buy a team just a few years ago. They got a whole bunch of stars—paid a whole bunch of money to them, and all of a sudden everybody gets a big head. Then they didn't make the playoffs; four years in a row.

So, where are the stars? *What happened to the stars?*

What happens? It's the thing that's beating in my chest; right here. It's the *heart*.

Some of them today say, *"Why bother? I'm making $8 million. I don't think I'll go into the corner and get hit. Why should I take a body check when I don't have to?"*

It makes you laugh.

That *never* happened to us. We weren't making that much. But that was our characteristic: character, character. That's what makes the team! The character; the people! You see?

When you've got the talent along *with* the character, you've got a good team. You stepped out confident of your ability and in the team and in what you're going to do. It's not a thrill. It's a job you have. You step on the ice because you have a job to do.

We had powerhouses. You know, one year in Detroit, 1951, we only lost 13 games; and another year, 1952, only 14! We had a power house. We won the Stanley Cup in 1950 and we won the Stanley Cup in 1952.

OPPOSITE: Leo Reise. (Courtesy of the *Windsor Star*)

When you win it there are no halos running around or streaks from heaven and what not. It was just you and the Cup. You finally got what you were after.

Euphoria sets in: "Great! We've done what we intended to do. We won; we beat them all. We're better than everybody else. Thank you very much."

And that's about all it is as far as I was concerned. That was the name of the game. That's what you're there for.

Of course, when we won the Stanley Cup, the next day you'd go down to the Olympia to get your things and it was, "So you won the Stanley Cup. See you next year. Don't ask for a raise." There were no parades. It was just, "See you next year." That's all there was to it.

All there was to it as far as the Detroit Red Wings were concerned was simply this: straightforward, headman the puck and go and get it and keep it in there; keep it in the attack zone. That's all there was to it.

I've always contended that the teams we had—in 1949-50, '51, and '52—were Carson Cooper's teams.

Jack Adams had all the input and managed the team and hired the coach and all that stuff, but he didn't pick the players.

Detroit had a great scout, Carson Cooper. *He* picked the players. In a sense, it was *his* team. Cooper picked the players; a lot of them, anyway.

He'd pick out a certain type of player: players with the hard work ethic, players with speed, players with size. Cooper's style of hockey was always straightforward. And that's the guys he'd pick: the ones who could headman the puck, the strong skaters. You didn't notice any little guys, small guys in Detroit. Except, maybe, Teddy Lindsay.

There were no dipsy-doodlers on *our* team. There were some good stick handlers, but nobody fiddled around too much. You shot the puck; you passed the puck and you got back where you belonged. And then you started over again. That was the Detroit Red Wings.

Powerful skaters and sound hockey players besides; simple reasons for our success. We were power skaters. We were all good skaters. They say that Montreal had a lot of skaters—that they were fast.

Well, we could skate with them and better them.

We were the best! What do you do for the encore? We were the best!

It didn't matter who it was.

We could out-skate anybody.

We could out-hit anybody.

We could out-score anybody.

Tommy Ivan was a fine coach. He coached me in Brantford, Junior B. He coached there and then he came up through the Detroit chain just like the rest of us, the hockey players, did. He had a very good formula for practices, a good concept of what was going on. We were pretty basic. They talk about these systems and what not. Tommy didn't have a system. His system was you played basic hockey. You backchecked, you were up and down and you headmanned the puck. The system was you moved the puck forward; you kept moving. If that's the system, then yes, we had a system. That was the formula he worked on. And he had the players put in his hands who could do it.

Our practices, we scrimmaged maybe the last 10 minutes, fiddle around. We'd split the team up between Westerners and Easterners, Catholics and Protestants, whatever it might be and have a little scrimmage, you know? The rest of the time was skating and drills. His practices were good practices. He kept you skating hard.

They always say you build a hockey team from the goal out, and in that sense; certainly we had a solid foundation. But this is one thing that gets me sometimes when I talk about the great goaltenders. We had a good goaltender in Terry Sawchuk, but he had the best defenseman in front of him. So, he'd better be a good goaltender!

Sawchuk had Hall of Fame guys playing defense in front of him the time he played in Detroit. He had Marcel Pronovost and Red Kelly and Black Jack Stewart; all in the Hall of Fame, and then me.

I'm not in the Hall of Fame, but I was a second-team All-Star in both 1950 and 1951. In those days in Detroit I was always on the ice at the start of a period and the end of a period. That was just normal practice. Our coach Tommy Ivan always said, "You don't want any goals scored early on you, and you don't want goals late. Late goals, they kill you at the end of a period." So, I always started the periods and ended the periods.

Bob Goldham's not in the Hall of Fame, but he was a sound defense man, too.

So, on defense in front of Sawchuk you had Kelly and I and Goldham and Pronovost and Benny Woit. That was the five of us. Benny was the fifth defenseman.

If Terry Sawchuk wasn't the best goaltender in those days, he never would be.

I always say, you should remember—when you start talking about how great these individuals were—to look at *the team*. It's a team!

Yes, you have to have a good goaltender, but you also have to have a good team to win the Stanley Cup. You can be the greatest goaltender in the world and end up in the bottom of the league.

We had good defense in front of the goaltender. And we had good back checkers for in front of the defensemen. As I said, you're a team!

It was just a solid, sound hockey club. They were all good guys. Detroit as a team was very close. We had a bunch of good guys. We stuck together. We had a lot of fun.

And we had a guy on our team named Gordie Howe. He was a teammate. He was a good guy; nice. Gordie didn't become a Catholic, but he could have, because he went to church with Teddy every day. They were very close, very close.

He was a powerhouse all by himself. When you play *with* a guy like Gordie, you really don't appreciate their total talent. You think, "Well, he's *supposed* to do that. That's what his job is. So sometimes you really don't appreciate how powerful he was and the plays he made. You'd see the great plays but that's routine. For him. For Gordie Howe.

Now, playing *against* Howe when I was with New York, well, he was an All-Star forward and I was an All-Star defenseman. We got along just fine.

Gordie, when he played, didn't go out of his way to injure, to elbow. When the opportunity arose and it looked like he was not being watched, he did it. Like when somebody's messing in the corner with him and starts to give it to him, he gave it *to them*—which is exactly what he's supposed to do. If he sees a guy with his head down, he nails him—which is exactly what he's supposed to do.

But, he never went out of his way to do it. That wasn't his style. He wasn't hunting for people to hit. He would never have gone and said, "Well, I'm going to hit Leo Reise. I'm going to put an elbow in his face," or something.

I was bigger than most of the players. Most of them were in the five-nine to six-foot range, but you got a few that were bigger. Like Howe's over six feet. Harry Watson was six feet. Bouchard was six foot something.

Size is always an advantage for a defenseman. It helps if you are big and strong and a powerful skater. But, you know, the little guys, the little stick handlers, like Edgar Laprade, Billy Taylor—that type of person, you had to be very careful with those guys. They give you the most trouble, those little guys. You were very cautious and wary of these people.

I was a hitter. I used to look for people with their heads down so I could nail them. So, when they were on the ice, they were looking for me, "Is Reise on the ice?" That was a big part of my game, to make sure they remember I'm on the ice.

The only thing I can't understand today is the boarding. They drive guys straight into the boards now. We got a boarding penalty for that. You can't hit straight into the boards. What I can't understand is players getting their elbows up and smashing the guy's head into the glass. Right now I think you see some vicious hockey. I don't think any of our guys went out to specifically hurt a guy. We don't play that way! That's *not* the way it was done!

One game we played in New York, and one of their star players just came back from being hurt. Jack Adams comes into the dressing room and says, "So and so was hurt. This is his first game back."

OPPOSITE: Leo Reise (Courtesy of Robert L. Wimmer)

We all just stared at him. *"What do you expect us to do? Hurt him?"*

We just looked at him, stared at him, and his face went red and he walked out of the room.

That's not the name of the game. We didn't play that game. Some of the other teams didn't care; no two ways about that. But we didn't. We didn't have to do that. I don't think any of us ever *thought* of doing it.

I never had a problem with Jack Adams; none at all. I didn't have to haggle with Jack over money. He knew what I could do. He knew what I could do. I got, as far as I was concerned, paid pretty well for it.

Of course, in one sense, it was one of the reasons I got traded after we won the Cup in 1952. Jack was a box-office type; a moneyman. At a certain range he said, "Well, I can save some money by moving this guy." That's a normal transaction. That's his business. I didn't resent the fact that he traded me. The only thing that was a little odd; I found out about it in the newspaper. A friend of ours called and said, "Did you know you are traded?"

Detroit never said, "Thank you very much. You did well for us," or anything like that. I never heard from them again. That sort of grabs you because you get attached to a team. Detroit is my home team! That was me! *I'm a Red Wing!* So, when they treat you like a *thing*, that sort of stings. But, that's all you expected. My father played in the NHL and he went through that and I expected it. But I thought at least they'd

say, even Tommy Ivan might say, "Hey, good luck in New York." There was none of that.

But, it was a great run. We had great teams then.

I went there in '46 at Christmas time. A little later on, Doug McCaig broke his leg and I played steadily after that.

Red Kelly came up the next year. In 1947, he started. We paired together. Once, when we played Toronto in the playoffs in 1950, even Connie Smythe, Maple Leafs Manager, said we were the best defensive pair in the NHL, Red Kelly and I.

That was a brutal series, you know, 1950. That was the semifinal against Toronto. That was a real tough, tough series. A brutal hockey series. There was a lot of body checking; a lot of hits and what not.

A lot of that was because of Gordie getting hurt in the first game, of course. It depends on who you talk to, who did what to whom, but I think Gordie just tripped and fell into the boards, but I don't know. I just know that something happened in front of our bench. Bang, he's down.

Then, of course, a melee started the next night. Lidio Fogolin knocked Toronto's Teeder Kennedy down. Teeder is the guy Gordie had been trying to check when he got hurt. Fogolin hit him real good and Kennedy was down.

I skated over and Kennedy hit me right in the forehead. That scar you see right between my eyes? That's the two-hander from Teeder

Kennedy. I swung back at him but I missed him and hit Jim Thompson. Ha, ha, ha.

Then we went into Toronto and one of the newspapermen said, "How come if Detroit is so dirty, *you* guys come in all bandaged up?"

Do you think Toronto wasn't dirty?

Let's put this on a level playing field. *Each was as bad as the next.* It was a memorable series, let's put it that way.

I scored the winning goal in Toronto in the fifth game in overtime. And in the seventh game I scored the winning goal in overtime. But, that was one of those anticlimaxes. I just shot the puck from the blue line and it just went in. Two bounces. Game over. That's finished.

The scoring of the goal was an anticlimax to the fact that we won the series; that we took them out of the playoffs after Toronto swept us in the Final in 1948 and 1949.

Then we beat the Rangers in seven games to win the 1950 Stanley Cup. They had Buddy O'Connor and Edgar Laprade. They had a really fine hockey club. Charlie Raynor was the goaltender. He was my goaltender when I played in the Navy. He was the one who said, "Leo, you can make the NHL! And don't let anybody tell you otherwise! "So, when I did turn pro, I was quite confident that I could handle the job.

It was either that or go back and become an accountant. I was a student accountant. So I decided I'd give hockey a try. It worked out grandly.

When I was 17, I started playing junior in Brantford. I had two or three years of junior "B" and we won the championship there. Then, the last year of junior, Detroit moved a farm club to Brantford and they started bringing players in.

I said, "Okay. You're paying them, I want to get paid."

Detroit said that they didn't know if I was going to make the team.

I said, "Then release me."

So I went to Guelph and played my last year of junior there. Then I went into the Navy. Our coach was an ex-Chicago man, Baldy Northcott. So, when I got out of the Navy, I turned pro with Chicago.

I played for the Kansas City Pla-Mors. That was a Chicago farm club. We won the championship there. I was on the first All-Star team that year.

I came up in January of '46 to fill in for the players who were hurt, and I made quite an impression with them then. As a matter of fact, the last game before they were going to send me down again, I was sitting at the end of the bench and Chicago Stadium started chanting, "We want Reise!"

So, finally Coach Johnny Gottselig put me out there and I went across the ice and nailed one of the New York Rangers we were playing against!

Anyway, I went down, but the next year I started with Chicago.

When I first came up in 1947, John Mariucci was my defense mate. John was my buddy. We got along famously.

The best fight I've ever seen was Mariucci and Black Jack Stewart. In Chicago, bare-knuckled, right out at center ice. Nobody grabbed anybody. Nobody was trying to pull the shirt over. Boom! Boom! And they fought in the penalty box. Oh, what a fight that was. You stood back and were thinking, "I'm glad it's not me." It was a great fight! Did they make a great pair when they fought. Oh, boy.

Mariucci was tough, but if anybody says he was the toughest guy in the league back then, it's only because they didn't know Black Jack Stewart that well. Jack Stewart was a great hockey player. He was my defense mate when I first went to Detroit, and man, he was tough.

In Chicago in the fall of 1946, I kept track of goals for and against. So when they decided they're going to send me down, I gave the general manager Bill Tobin and Gottselig the piece of paper I'd been tracking the goals on and I said, "This doesn't look too bad. We're the best defense pair you have." So, they kept me up, but only for a while.

Detroit had that farm club in Brantford, as I mentioned, and I was on their Negotiation List—the players Detroit owned—off and on all the time. I went to Detroit's training camps as a Junior. When Detroit found I could play in the NHL, they said, "We want you back."

So in December, I got traded to Detroit. I got a letter from Tobin saying they were sorry to let me go, but that they, Detroit, want you back.

It was like going home, really, because I'd been to their training camps and I knew a lot of the guys and what not.

After I got traded to Detroit, me and Mariucci ran into each other in the corner. Bang! And he came out swinging. Then he said, "Oh, it's you!" He picked up his stick and skated away. He was my friend. I'm glad he didn't carry on because he would have torn me apart! No maybe about it, either. He was tough.

As far as me going to Jack Adams because our playoff shares were light one year, well, Lindsay mentions that somewhere but I'm afraid I have no recollection of that. You have to remember, I was gone from Detroit after the 1952 season. I never saw what the players shares were when Detroit won those other Stanley Cups in 1954 and 1955.

Teddy sometimes is bitter about the NHL. I was treated well. I have no complaints whatsoever. I was treated well by Detroit, then I went to New York and I was treated well by New York. I have no axe to grind with the NHL. They treated me well and that's just fine. Thank you very much. So I kind of resent sometimes when people talk about how they did this and that.

I honestly believe that the Players Association started with the NHL Pension Society. You had three players from each of the teams on the Pension Board. So, we'd have a meeting. So, here are all these guys together. Then they started talking about other things other than pensions. It was a logical extension. And that was the foundation, actually, of the union because everybody was talking to everybody, which had *never* happened before. No, it never happened before.

Because you hated them. Definitely. You never talked to the competitors; you never saw them except on the ice. Gaye Stewart lives close to here, and just two years ago I went with him to a Toronto Maple Leafs alumni dinner. Gaye was a teammate in Detroit for a year and he played for the Leafs, too. I look around the room, all these Maple Leafs you know, and I thought, "What am I doing here? These are *the enemy*. I'm sitting in the midst of the enemy!" I hadn't played a game in the National Hockey League in almost *50 years,* and it was still the feeling you had. You never got friendly with them.

But when they started the NHL Pension Society, then all of a sudden these people would be together and then you could talk to the other guy and the other guy and the other guy. Which Lindsay did, of course.

People squawk about the pension program. I was in on that right from the start. You could take your pension when you were 45. Well, some of the guys took their pension when they were 45 while they were still playing hockey and still working. They had no reason to take it then! They could leave it with us until they were 65 or whatever. So, they get peanuts at 45. If they would have left it in until they were 65 they'd get three times or four times as much! But they squawk about it because it was so little. But cer-

tainly it was so little! They mismanaged it. I resent that, because the NHL pension program was never meant to be a lifetime-type of pension. It was expected that you would only work so long in the NHL—until you were 32; 35 max. Then you'd go out and get a job and your job would have a pension and the NHL pension would just be supplementary to that.

But, if you expected to live on it, you weren't going to do it! It was never intended to do that! This is where there's a conflict. People squawk about it.

When you leave hockey, you leave hockey. Period. Those things and those people; they're in the past. You move on; move on. I've been in three careers. I was in hockey, in plumbing wholesaling, and in the plastic business. You move on.

Still, you're identified—no matter what you did since—as a Red Wing. You're an NHL player. When I meet somebody it's, "You're the NHL hockey player."

They didn't say what you did in plumbing or what you did in plastics; it's "You're the NHL hockey player." They never forget it.

Like I said, it was a great run. We had great teams then.

Good memories, good memories. I had a good run of it. It was a good career. I've never been back. I have no regrets.

MARTY PAVELICH

"BLACKIE"

DETROIT RED WINGS 1947-1957

STANLEY CUP 1950, 1952, 1954, 1955

MAYBE SOMEWHERE ALONG the trail I might run into Jack Adams again and I'll ask him some of these questions.

Jack would have been a good interview for you:

"Why'd you do this and why did you do that?"

"Why did you break up such a great team?"

Maybe he had to. Maybe the owner, Mr. Norris, said, "You have to do it."

I have no idea.

I made the Red Wings when I was 19, in the fall of 1947. I was a Red Wing for 10 years. We played in the Stanley Cup Final seven times. And we won the Stanley Cup four times, in 1950, '52, '54 and '55.

Detroit was in the playoffs every year I was a Red Wing, and I played in 91 of a possible 93 playoff games in my career.

I didn't miss too many in the regular season, either. The most games I ever had to sit out in any one season were six. Some years I'd play them all. Others, I might miss two or three.

We won the regular season in 1956-57, making it eight regular-season championships in nine years for Detroit. But in that spring of 1957, Boston beat us in five games in the first round, ending our streak of three straight appearances in the Stanley Cup Final.

Less than five months later, I wasn't a Red Wing anymore.

OPPOSITE: Marty Pavelich. (Courtesy of the *Windsor Star*)

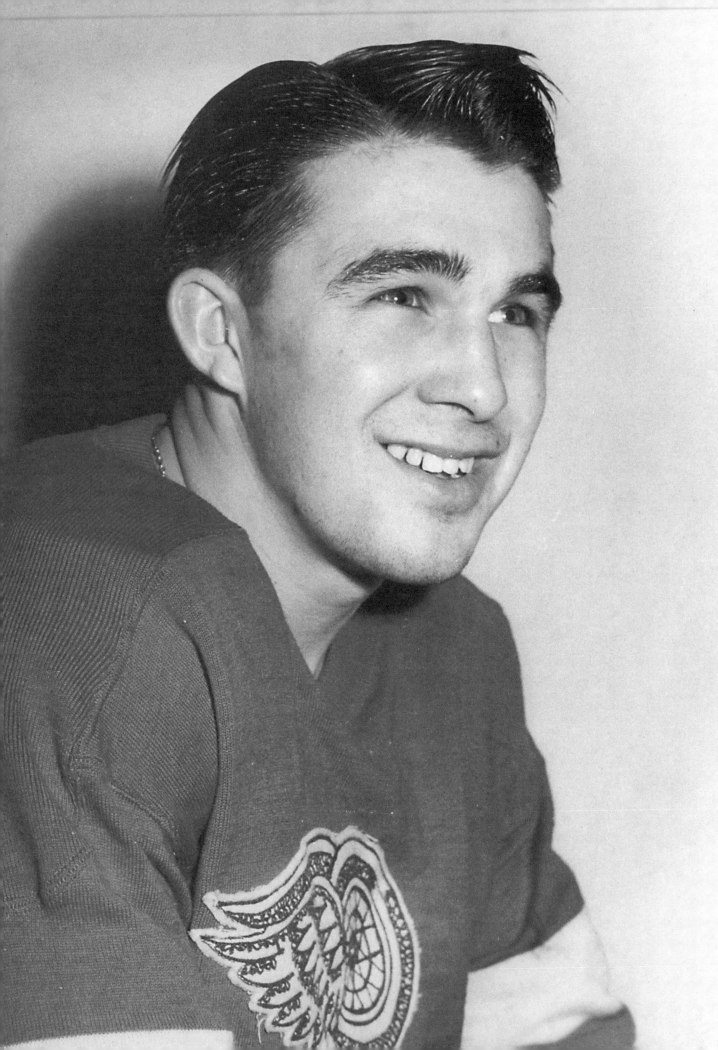

In fact, I wasn't even a professional hockey player anymore.

I remember that summer. I went out to Jackson Hole, Wyoming, in a brand-new 1957 DeSoto convertible I'd just bought.

We drove out there and I came back a little early just because I had to see Jack Adams. We had come back just before training camp.

So I went in to see him up in his office in the front of Olympia Stadium, and we talked and Jack said, "I tried to trade you, but nobody wanted you. So, I'm sending you to the minors."

I said, "Jack, you're not sending me anywhere. I'm all done."

I was sitting in the big leather chair in his office, and I gave him a backhanded wave.

I said, "I'm done."

I walked out and he got mad because he wasn't getting another body; he wasn't getting any money and all this stuff.

I was stunned, no doubt about it.

After all, I'd been in the Detroit organization since I was 16. That's where we first came! That's who scouted us! That's who brought us here! Detroit is where you want to be.

Two or three weeks later, a friend of ours who was very involved with certain individuals in the National Hockey League came up to me and said, "Marty, are you interested in coming back with Boston or Chicago or New York?" They were all interested in me at that time.

I said, "No. I'm all done. I've made the cut. Now is the time to get out."

I didn't want to play anyplace else! No place else! It was the only place I ever wanted to play. I was going to finish my career in Detroit. That's why I made my stand.

I could have stayed another three or four years, I think. If Sid Abel would have been coaching at that time—Sid brought Teddy Lindsay back—I think I could have played, too.

I was only 29 years old. I was very young at that time. It was tough. It was very tough.

The next two seasons out of hockey just about killed me. The thing that saved me is I was so damn busy trying to make a living that I didn't go to that many games.

It was tough for a couple of years. The guys don't call you. They want to keep a distance away from you because Adams didn't want us around. So, those guys didn't want to invite you to games or go out to lunch with you. That wasn't right.

Lucky that it worked out, or whatever, but it worked out. I had enough confidence in myself to make it work out in the business world. So, I look back on all that and maybe it was a blessing in disguise. Because I was young enough to get out of hockey and get into the business world.

The Red Wings' home ice was at Olympia Stadium. (Courtesy of Robert L. Wimmer)

I love hockey. When I look back on being a Red Wing, all I can say is that it was great. It was great. I have no regrets.

I'm really thrilled to have played in the NHL. I'm happy about being a Red Wing. I'm a Red Wing all over.

It was a *great* time to be a hockey player in the NHL!

I was 16 when I went to my first Red Wings training camp. That was the fall of 1944.

They sent me to Galt in the Ontario Hockey Association.

Gordie Howe and I were on the Galt Red Wings together for the 1944-45 season, sort of.

Gordie couldn't play in any games. Because of a technicality, I guess you'd say. Jack Adams couldn't get Gordie's transfer out of western Canada. Adams could only get one transfer for a Junior player from western Canada—like Gordie from Saskatchewan—to play in the Ontario Hockey Association, and he used that for a guy named Terry Cavanaugh. Adams couldn't get another transfer for Gordie, so Gordie just sat.

Gordie was skating every day because we practiced every day, but Gordie could only play in exhibition games. We only played a few exhibition games, not too many, so Gordie just sat there for the whole year.

Does that sound like a *mistake* to you?

The best hockey player *ever*, a guy who wants to play and he can't play for a whole season because Jack or whoever in the front office made a mistake and couldn't get him a transfer.

It was very hard on Gordie.

I suppose it was also very hard on Gordie that that's the only year we were teammates where I scored more goals than him! I suppose that's right, yes. It's in the record book. I had eight goals for the Galt Red Wings in 1944-45. Gordie, since he didn't appear in any games, he didn't score any goals. I've never thought of that before.

I had three good Junior years in Galt. Then Jack Adams asked me if I wanted to turn pro and I said, "Hell, yes!"

That was in the spring of 1947. Gordie had just finished his first year in the National League.

Gordie played in the minors, in the United States Hockey League for the Omaha Knights, the year after he sat out when we were both in

Galt. Then he was with Detroit the next year, 1946-47.

We were still pretty good buddies. We'd stayed in touch.

I told him Jack wanted to sign me, and Gordie said, "Hey, go to Omaha. There are a lot of good-looking girls down there."

Instead, I went home to the Soo—Sault Ste. Marie, Ontario—and I worked out all summer—construction work and everything else. I skated all the time, and I was in great shape when I came into camp.

I darn near made the big team right off the bat in the fall of 1947.

I never did make it to Omaha. They sent me to the Indianapolis Capitals in the American Hockey League.

Adams had changed his mind right at the end of camp and had actually decided to keep me, but it was too late. I was already gone to Indianapolis. I had to stay down for a month. Then they brought me up.

Except for half a dozen games in Indianapolis the following season, I never went back to the minors. I played the rest of my career in Detroit.

When I broke into the NHL, it was an era where a lot of us came out of the Depression. Then they had the second World War.

A lot of guys who came back from the war years, they were there in '47. Plus, you had the guys who had filled in during the war. It was really a tremendous mixture on the teams at that time.

Jack Stewart, who I just think the world of, was a great defensemen.

Sid Abel, he was a great captain. I sat beside him for quite a few years because we went by our numbers. He was 12 and I was 11. He was just a great leader.

Gordie Howe was just fun. I enjoyed Gordie very much. Not just playing with him. We went fishing together, we knocked around together.

The guys used to call the four of us—Red Kelly, Ted Lindsay, Gordie and myself—"The Dead-End Kids," from the movies. We were always together, the four of us. We did everything together. Dancing, dating, the whole darn thing.

You know what? Teddy was—off the ice, you know—*the nicest guy*. God, he's a Jekyll and Hyde.

Teddy was just a *tremendous* competitor. He's a little guy, a little-guy complex or something, but he was a real competitor.

I will tell you this: If 15 guys were going to kick the hell out of me, Ted Lindsay was the guy I wanted with me. We're going down, but by God we're going to take a few, too!

He's always been that way. He's a competitor—fire-hearted. That's just his nature. He's a great, great competitor.

He just would battle, no matter who or no matter what. He's been hit sometimes and punched pretty hard by a few people, but he got more than his share of licks in.

Teddy was good for Gordie. He pushed Gordie at first.

Gordie, when he first came, was an easygoing type of young guy. Everybody used to think he was lazy when he first started because he had those long strides and so forth. You just couldn't catch him, that's all!

When he saw Teddy start roughing up a few people and so forth, not letting guys take advantage of him, I think Gordie picked that up.

Gordie was tough, tough. He was as tough as anybody I've ever known in our era. He was so strong: 18-inch neck and big arms.

And big fists. Yeah, he could throw 'em with the best. I never saw him lose a fight. I never saw him come close. I would say guys on other teams were afraid of him, yes.

There were more fights when we played, but in those days, I don't ever remember—in all the years I played—ever running a guy from behind. Never!

That was a *gutless* thing to do. Never run a guy from behind!

I never took a stick and crosschecked a guy from behind into the boards; didn't do that.

But did we ever have bodychecks! Oh, man! You don't see any of those bodychecks now! You see bodychecks along the *boards*—along the *boards*! And the way they are running guys from behind today!

Our bodychecks were out in center ice! If you got your head down and you got hit, that was your own stupidity. If a guy threw a puck up the boards or whatever, and you looked down for the puck, but you know a guy is coming at you, that was just tough.

Some of those guys! All of a sudden you'd get hit by somebody like Jack Stewart.

Those were balcony jobs! He hit 'em so hard; they'd be gone—up in the balcony! That's the thing that you don't see today. You don't see the open-ice hitting.

You had your share of fights. You had your share of the good checking. But not the dirty stuff.

I mean, God darn it, these hits from behind! I thought they wouldn't stop what they were doing until we had a couple of guys become paraplegics.

Then I thought they might see the light and say, "All right, we're going to start calling this."

I just got fed up with the way they were calling the penalties, and *not* calling the penalties, for the last many, many years.

There wasn't as much grabbing and holding and interfering in our times; just a little. We might cut in, in certain spots, and just slow you up for a second, but then you were out of there.

Now, cripes, they grab you, put a lasso on you, and it's getting way out of hand. The interference—the grabbing, the holding—you're really eliminating the talent of some of the players.

The guy that's just hanging in there—he grabs and holds and so forth, and he keeps a job. That, I don't agree with.

Hockey is so different now than how we did it. Now, they're all over the ice. They're going all in different directions. They're playing man-to-man.

That's *kind* of what we did, too. A lot of the game of hockey is the same. I mean, you can't change the game a heck of a lot.

We played such a positional thing. You played your wing, up and down, circle to circle. So the game *is* different.

We were good at both ends. And we could score some goals.

We used to shoot it in; we invented it, that's right. But we had the power type of teams that could do that. In 1952-53, for example, we scored almost a goal a game more than any other team in the NHL. We scored 222 goals that season. Chicago came second to us with 169— 63 fewer than we scored in 70 games.

OPPOSITE: Red Wings coach Tommy Ivan, left, looks over the Madison Square Garden rink in New York with Bob Goldham and Marty Pavelich. (AP/WWP)

When we shot the puck in, the first guy in always went and he took the man out. Because when you throw that puck around pretty hard, that defenseman has a tough time getting control of it. He's got his back turned to you. The first guy took the man, the second guy picked up the puck. That was the way that went.

Then what happened, Jacques Plante came into the picture and that changed that.

Jacques Plante, the Hall of Fame goalie for the Canadiens. He broke in with Montreal in 1953. He put his name on the Stanley Cup six times in Montreal.

Plante was the first goalie to wear a facemask—the guy who *invented* the facemask for goalies, in 1959.

Johnny Wilson used to tell us that he and his brother Larry—Larry, God bless him, was my teammate three seasons in Detroit—they grew up playing baseball in Quebec with Jacques Plante. He was a catcher. So it stood to reason that he'd invent the facemask. He was used to it from baseball.

I'm sure Plante and Doug Harvey—one of the best defensemen of all time—they got together in Montreal.

Every time we played Montreal, if Harvey was out of the lineup, we knew we could beat them because he meant that much to that team. He was a real general back there on the blue line. Doug Harvey was beautiful to watch. He would just slow the game down, and he'd make it go

the way *he* wanted it to go. He was great! Not the greatest skater, but the way he could pass and control and things, it was beautiful.

But, Plante and Doug Harvey; they got together in Montreal, and that's where that started—the goalie leaving the net to stop the puck behind the goal.

When the goaltender started to go and stop it behind the net, the defenseman no longer had to stop to pick up the puck. He could pick it up on the fly then.

Now, I will say this: One thing that I *do* like now—you're starting to see people with ability. You've got some talented, talented guys on the ice today.

That's what we had. We had a lot of guys who had talent—that skating ability, that stick-handling ability.

The game is very fast, and then you see a guy like Sergei Fedorov! I mean, he's worth the price of admission. I mean, he puts on a show. He's an outstanding hockey player!

You've got a guy with a heart as big as a mountain like Stevie Yzerman. Certain people have determination to a certain point, and then they quit. Stevie goes beyond that; he goes beyond that.

I love the guy. I've been involved with him in a couple of charity projects, and he's just a classy young man.

He could have played in our day. Chris Chelios could have played; Nicklas Lidstrom could have played; Brendan Shanahan could have played; Luc Robitaille; Brett Hull.

But they would have to check, and they wouldn't have gotten the goals they get now.

In our day, Teddy and Gordie worked great as a unit.

They may not be speaking to each other now, or whatever, but that line was just a *hell* of a line.

They were inseparable. My gosh! Gordie *lived* with Teddy at his mom and dad's house.

It's hard to believe they're not speaking to each other now. That goes back; it started with the Players' Association. Then it just grew from there.

It's foolish. It's sad. Let's leave it at that. It's really sad because they are two great hockey players. Two great men.

The two most colorful hockey players in all the years I played were Rocket Richard and Ted Lindsay. They could electrify a crowd.

People wanted to kill Lindsay!

People wanted to kill Richard!

The greatest goal scorer of all time—they can talk about Wayne Gretzky; they can talk about Howe; they can talk about Mario Lemieux. *But*

it has to be Richard. The guy was just a fierce, fierce competitor.

When this man got over the blue line, he was going one place—and one place only—and that was for the net. And he was going to get that shot on the net.

I have nothing, *nothing* but great respect for that man as a hockey player. We became pretty good friends later in life, too. I was a big, big fan of his.

I checked him for 10 years. That was my job, to stop Rocket Richard.

Gordie Howe was a very, very strong man. Rocket Richard was just as strong. The forearms on him, and the arms on him, were just unbelievable.

He was coming around the net one night and I hit him pretty good. I cut him just a little bit over the eye. Not intentionally, but whatever part of my head or my shoulder hit him, cut him.

He was madder than hell. He was going to clobber me. I mean, he was mad.

He ran me, and then *he* got a penalty. So, I'm giving it to him, "You dumb Frenchman!" You this, you that! I'm really going at him.

He goes into the penalty box—and Teddy Lindsay, Gordie Howe and those guys are on the power play.

As soon as The Rocket comes back out on the ice, my job is to get on the ice.

I'll never forget, Bobby Goldham, God bless him, is in our end, and he's throwing the puck up to me and he hollers, "Look out! Duck!"

I *just saw* Richard out of the corner of my eye. He came out of the penalty box and he was going to really drill me. His stick scraped the top of my head because I ducked in the nick of time. Thank God for that; thank God for Bob Goldham.

Bobby Goldham should be in the Hockey Hall of Fame. I tried to get him in. One *hell* of a defenseman! We got him from Chicago in the off season after we won the Cup in 1950.

That summer, I was up in the Soo and I said to my mom, "You know what? That guy is going to really be a big help to us."

He came, and he wasn't playing much when he first got here. Then somebody got hurt and they started to play him, and *nobody* took his job after that. He was one hell of a defenseman.

Anyway, after that close call with The Rocket, I said, "You know, this is ridiculous. I can't carry on this way."

So, *I started to kid with him.*

I scored a goal one night against him and I said, "Rocket, look out! I'm hot tonight!"

He'd laugh like hell! He'd get the biggest kick out of that. Then he'd get to the point where there were times where he had me lined up and he'd go right by.

He and I became pretty good buddies after that. I checked him, checked him, and checked him—just like I was supposed to; hard, but nothing ever dirty or anything else.

And I'd be kidding him a lot, too. So, that's the way it went with The Rocket.

We were the first team to have a checking line. So, while it was my job to stop Richard, it was our line's job to stop the other team's best line.

Our Coach, Tommy Ivan, was the guy who started that checking line routine.

Tommy Ivan was the guy who started "the box" for killing penalties in your own end.

Tommy Ivan was a neat guy. He did a *great* job. Tommy coached us for seven years, and we made it into the Stanley Cup Finals five times!

Tommy Ivan's another thing. Tommy left here, and it was just that he and Adams saw things in different ways.

Tommy married, and Jack didn't know about it. That's what I hear the story was.

If we wouldn't have lost him, we might have won a few more Stanley Cups. I think we *would* have won if he'd have stayed.

Jack Adams just gave it up—the coaching—the year before I came in. Jack had been coach of the Detroit Red Wings *for 20 years*.

Jack stayed on, of course, as the manager.

Jack Adams and Gordie Howe. (Courtesy of Robert L. Wimmer)

So, Tommy Ivan's first season as a coach in the NHL was my rookie season, 1947-48.

Tommy was our coach when we won the Cup in 1950, 1952 and 1954. Too bad Tommy's gone.

Tommy might have talked Jack into not making that Lindsay trade to Chicago. He might

have been able to control the situation and carry her on. But when he got out of there. . .

It was tough, tough on the coach, to have Adams sitting right behind our bench. He'd be hollering at the players, the coach, the referee—anybody!

I remember one night we were playing the New York Rangers and we got a penalty. In those days when you score a goal—rather, when you *give up a goal*—you still had to kill your full time.

Camille Henry—just a little whisper of an individual—goes out there and poof! He scores a goal. I was killing the penalty at that time.

Adams growls: "Pull him off! Pull Pavelich off! Put out Lindsay and Howe!"

So, Tommy sends out Lindsay and Howe.

Boom! Camille gets another one!

Now, you hear Adams yelling, "Pull them off! Pull them off!"

Everybody on the bench, we wanted to look back and say, "*Now* who the hell do you want us to put on?"

But, Tommy had a way.

Say you are playing and you're having a rough time right now, or even if you're not having a rough time. Say you were playing pretty well.

But Jack's on your ass.

You'd hear him yell, "Get Pavelich off! Get him off!"

Then we'd go on the road. And we'd play maybe three games on the road; go to New York, go to Boston, go to Montreal, and come home.

Tommy had to call Jack after every game, and, of course, Jack would ask, "Who played well tonight?"

Tommy would say, "Marty Pavelich had *a hell* of a night!"

You only had a *fair* night, but Tommy Ivan would tell Jack, "He played his best game of the season! He was *outstanding*!"

The next night, same thing. Jack would ask, "Who played well?"

Tommy'd say, "Marty Pavelich! Oh, man, I mean, he was terrific!"

So, by the time we came back home, Jack's all excited. He *can't wait* to see you!

And then it would be somebody else's turn.

Benny Woit, or he'd get down on Metro Prystai every once in a while—a lot of guys. That's the way Jack went. He really intimidated some individuals, too, who played on our teams.

You took it. You took it. I did. If you came to me, I'd get mad. Then I'd go out and prove you wrong. I would just say, "The hell with that. I'm going to be tougher than that. I'm not going to let you beat me."

That's the way Marty Pavelich has been all his life. I'm a positive thinker and I just say, "You're not going to beat me."

But other guys, you'd shout at and they'd go right in the tank for you. There's nothing left.

You couldn't understand it.

When we won, it was *his team*.

When we lost, it was *our team*.

I remember when I first came in; guys were saying this and that about things Jack Adams would do, and so forth and so on. I heard it *before* I even got there to Detroit. You talk to guys.

Everybody said Jack had *always* been the same way.

He was a bull in a china shop.

He was a tough hombre.

When I did get to Detroit, then I understood why those guys felt the way they felt about Jack Adams. He demanded every bit of loyalty out of every one of us.

Tommy Ivan always used to say, "If you've got the horses to pull the load, the job's easy."

And he said, "The teams we had, we had the horses to get the job done."

Tommy coached us into the Stanley Cup Final each of our first two years in Detroit, in 1948 and in 1949.

Toronto swept us four straight both years to win the Stanley Cup. And they outscored us, 30-12, in doing it.

Turk Broda, the Toronto netminder, was unbelievable. In the '48 Final, he had a goals-against average of 1.75. In the '49 Final, it was 1.16!

Then, in 1950, we met Toronto again—this time in the first round.

Of course, that was the year Gordie got hurt in the first game of that series against Toronto.

Oh sure, I was there.

Gordie was just going along the boards between the two benches, and Teeder Kennedy came back to check him and brought his stick up, and Gordie went down for the count.

I don't think Kennedy *deliberately* went at him that way, but we all thought, "Gee, Gordie is going to die." We were all *that* concerned.

They took him over to Harper Hospital, not too far from the Olympia, and the neurosurgeon happened to be in the hospital at the time, so they were able to take Gordie into surgery and take care of him right away.

Close to dawn the following morning, we got the word that Gordie was going to be all right.

At that time, we all thought it was deliberate, so we got into a big brawl with Toronto the next night at the Olympia. We were still all excited; all mad and so forth.

That year, 1950, we beat Toronto in seven games in that first-round playoff.

Leo Reise scored in overtime in Game 4 to even the series at two wins apiece and prevent us from falling behind three games to one.

Then, in Game 7 at the Olympia, Radar did it again. Leo's second overtime goal of the series beat Toronto, 1-0.

Toronto had won three Cups in a row, and they wound up winning it again in 1951, so who knows?

Maybe Leo Reise kept the Leafs from winning five straight Stanley Cups with that goal. Good.

You know what? Every time we played Toronto or Montreal in those days, *we would have played for nothing*, because we hated each other. We *hated* Toronto and Montreal.

Those back-to-back games were just out of this world. You played Saturday in Montreal and Sunday in Detroit.

On the overnight train back to Detroit after the game at The Forum on Saturday night, Jack would come through, and then all of a sudden, he'd go in his compartment and he'd stay there.

We'd stay up. We used to always have a couple of beers after the game, and we'd stay up, tell stories and laugh. We'd go over the game, over and over. That was the nice part of it.

I'd stay up for an hour or so until I cooled down. You couldn't play cards because our berths would be all made up by then. So you'd cool down and have a couple of beers and go to bed, and get back in the next afternoon and have a bite to eat, have a little rest, and play 'em again that night at Olympia Stadium. That was a fun thing.

They used to have the dining car and the two sleeping cars; one for Montreal, one for Detroit.

Well, then we got into a little bit of a scuffle—maybe a couple of scuffles—on the train one night.

Then what they had to do was, they had to put the dining car in the middle and the other sleeping car on the back so we didn't have to walk through each other's car on the train anymore.

Say the night before, in Montreal, you had a tough game. Maybe you got in a fight or something like that. Well, there'd been a little shouting back and forth, and you just didn't *want* to go through the other team's car. You just didn't want to. You didn't even want to say hello to them.

Today, everybody talks to everybody.

In our day, no way, you didn't talk to them. You just didn't. You didn't want to. Funny, but that's true. You just didn't. Bragging rights all summer, going home to Canada, were at stake.

You go back home, and all those Canadians—all those Montreal fans, all those Toronto fans—and you had the bragging rights because you were the Stanley Cup champions!

I found out just how nice *that* was for the first time in 1950 because, of course, we went on and we won it; we beat New York Rangers in a Game 7 Final. A double-overtime Game 7!

They damn near beat us, you know? They just hung in there and kept battling and battling, but finally we beat them.

We played the first game at the Olympia—which we won—and then the next two games at Maple Leaf Gardens in Toronto, which we split. The circus came into Madison Square Garden, so the Rangers couldn't play any games in the Final there. The last four games were at Olympia Stadium, at home.

They beat us, 3-1, in Toronto in Game 2 before Harry Lumley shut them out, 4-0, there in Game 3.

So we came home, up two games to one. That's when New York beat us twice in a row in overtime at Olympia! Bones Raleigh scored both the overtime goals.

We were down, three games to two.

We went down to Toledo and stayed at the Secor Hotel. Jack always took us down there during the playoffs. That was a nice hideout.

We were down there, and we all went out together. That's the thing we always did. If you didn't drink, that was fine, but you threw a dollar in the pot like everybody else.

We'd sit around and I'd say to one of my linemates, "Darn it, why weren't you going tonight? What was wrong? What was this? Why did that happen?"

Or one of them would say, "Marty, what the hang's wrong? Why weren't *you* going tonight?"

You'd sit around talking; we'd work things out. We were that close.

This night in the 1950 Final, Black Jack Stewart got into a couple of beers, and he was mad because the big line wasn't going. Howe was hurt, and that left Lindsay and Abel. I'll never forget it. Oh, he was mad at Sid.

He said, "Damn it! If you don't get those kids going, I am going to kick the bleep out of *you*! *And* those two kids!"

And then he grabbed the wrong raincoat and stormed out. Nobody questioned him. Nobody said a word.

The next morning, we're all waiting for the bus on the steps of the hotel. We were going to the Mud Hens ballgame.

Everybody asked—because he and Jack roomed together, "Sid, how'd you sleep?"

Sid said, "Well, I slept with one eye open all night!"

We beat Rangers, 5-4, in Game 6 to force Game 7, and Pete Babando scored in *double overtime* to win the 1950 Stanley Cup.

We won it again in 1952, the year we won it in eight straight.

We had to play the first two games against Montreal in the Final away from home because there was a circus or something at Olympia Stadium. And it was our home-ice advantage!

But we went to The Forum and beat the Canadiens, 3-1 and 2-1, and Montreal never scored another goal in the series!

1952 was the first time Montreal had ever been swept in any playoff series.

Montreal's been a Stanley Cup finalist 31 times. We are still the only team—to this day—to *sweep the Canadiens* in a Stanley Cup Final!

That was after we swept Toronto, 4-0, in the first round in 1952. It was the first time the Maple Leafs had ever been swept in a playoff series—best-of-seven, anyway.

Terry Sawchuk didn't give up a goal at Olympia Stadium in the entire 1952 playoffs.

That team in 1951-52! We could have *played all summer* and never lost!

The chemistry was just wonderful! We would just kick the hell out of anybody we played! And we proved it.

I look back on those seven straight league championships—seven in a row from 1948-49 through 1954-55; then we came second in the National Hockey League in 1955-56; then we finished first again in 1956-57.

So it was eight regular-season championships in nine years!

That tells you what kind of team we had every year.

And then Jack would do things sometimes that just didn't work out. I mean, we'd give so much talent away!

At one time, Adams wanted to trade—I remember he talked to a few of us—he wanted to trade Sawchuk.

He was mad at Sawchuk.

Sawchuk is the greatest goaltender of all time, bar none. I don't care who is playing today, or who is breaking records. Don't get me wrong. I mean, they will break his records, but they'll never be as great as that guy is.

I sat by him in the dressing room. He was a very moody type of guy. He would say hello and then he wouldn't say hello, and then he'd be a lot of fun. He'd go in streaks. Terry used to drink a little bit, and I think his moods fluctuated a little bit because of that.

Terry was terrible in practice. He hated practice. I guess all goaltenders did.

You look at those guys now, and I look at the equipment that they have, and what Terry and those guys had.

It was all felt. And then they had the arm pads, and they were all felt. No protection at all. No wonder they hated practice.

But he was a really, really outstanding goaltender. When he got into a game, he was a hell of a competitor!

The thing that set Terry Sawchuk apart was his super, super hands. Man, did he have a pair of hands! His catching hand was so fast! That's because he was a ballplayer. He had great hands and he was very quick. He'd challenge you. He'd challenge you all the time.

But, Adams got mad at him.

There was a chance Montreal wanted him. And we were going to get Harvey.

If we'd have gotten Doug Harvey, and we had Glenn Hall, we'd have been very, very tough to beat.

Well, Jack didn't make the deal for Harvey, but he did go ahead and ship Sawchuk to Boston after we won the Cup in 1955.

That was our last Stanley Cup.

When Tommy left for Chicago to coach after we won the Stanley Cup in 1954, we got Jimmy Skinner as our new coach, and Jimmy—I like Jimmy very much as a person, I like him *very much*—but I think Jimmy was too close to Jack. He really believed in Jack.

When we won that last Cup in 1955, we used to have a lot of meetings among ourselves. Jimmy coached, but the players—I mean, we had confidence and all that stuff in Jimmy, and, of course, with Jack—but Skinner was so close to Jack that we just kind of took over a little control there.

Glenn Hall replaced Sawchuk. Hall led the NHL in shutouts with 12 that first season in Detroit. Glenn was a hang of a goaltender. He's a Hall of Famer and all of that—Mr. Goalie.

We had him for only the two years, 1955-56 and 1956-57. He was an All-Star both seasons!

Hall made a comment to Jack one time that got him traded away.

Jack said, "Now don't tell anybody about your contract."

Hall said, "Mr. Adams, I won't. I'm too ashamed to."

After that, he was *gone*.

Adams traded Hall to Chicago along with Teddy Lindsay the same summer—1957, that he tried to send me to the minors.

We had talented kids. The Red Wings were—we were—so great in that era that a lot of kids in Canada started to want to play in Detroit. Not in Montreal or in Toronto; they wanted to play in Detroit!

Our farm system was really loaded with a lot of talent, and then all of a sudden, Adams started to give them away.

We gave away so many good players; gone to other clubs. And a lot of times we were trading away really good talent and getting back nothing in return.

I mean, a perfect example is John Bucyk.

Adams trades Bucyk to Boston in July, 1957, straight-up for Terry Sawchuk, because Hall is gone and now he needs a goalie.

So, he goes and he gets Terry back, for Johnny Bucyk.

Bucyk had been with us for a season and a half. He was just coming off his first full year in the NHL with Detroit. He was 22 when Jack traded him.

Johnny Bucyk, "Chief," played for *21 years* for Boston after that and scored 545 goals! That's still Boston's all-time record, by the way. More than Phil Esposito, Bobby Orr, or any of those guys with Boston.

I mean, *come on*! We could have, we would have, won another two or three Stanley Cups if we didn't trade all those players away.

Red Kelly should have never left here. There's another guy that should have never left.

See, if Red would have stayed, if Teddy would have stayed, if I would have stayed, we had that chemistry still there—still there!

Instead of losing to Toronto, as Detroit did in both the 1963 and 1964 Finals, we would have won it! Hell, yes! *Yes!*

Red goes to Toronto, laughing like hell, like he should be. Detroit was where he belonged! It was his everything!

We gave away a brand-new Cadillac and got back a Chevy. I mean, I like Mark Reaume—the guy we got for Red from Toronto—but there's no comparison, *no way*!

Red goes over there and he wins four more Stanley Cups. Shoot, *we* could have won those. That just grinds the living—that's what gets me mad more than anything.

It was just a lot of trades that went crazy, and it is too bad. We lost the chemistry on that team! That would be the one thing, while I look back, that I get a little mad about.

No way were we heading downhill after the 1956-57 season when he got rid of Teddy, Hall, and me. No! Oh, no! No! We finished first in the regular season that year, don't forget.

We still had a great nucleus. If we'd have kept Teddy and myself and a few of the guys, we would've been in contention right along!

Everything I did in hockey I applied in the business world: You've got a commitment, you've got dedication, you've got loyalty. You've got all those things.

Teddy and I started our own plastics company. I wanted to work for myself. That's how Ted and I got started. We made parts for the automobile industry. I had a rough time for five years; five years. I didn't put a red cent in the bank. But, it came after that and did very well, and we built a pretty good-sized company. We had about 90 people working for us. Now, I've been retired 10 years, and it worked out very good. I really, really loved the business world. I enjoyed it much more than the hockey.

The thing that really developed my business was the same thing that made us a winning team:

chemistry. You've got to have chemistry! You've got to trust each other. We lost that in Detroit.

Jack would bring some guys up from the minors to fill in, and so forth, and the chemistry was gone. We work all year to get there to the playoffs, and then he'd put someone else in there, and it just didn't work.

But it was an era of—well, let's just say I don't begrudge it. The only thing I begrudge is not winning more Stanley Cups.

Jack Adams started to do things to *me* down the stretch in my last season, 1957; after we announced the formation of the NHL Players Association.

I couldn't get on the ice a few times. The crowds at Olympia Stadium—I had a real following here—the fans would holler for me and cheer for me, and so they would throw me out every once in a while.

The first part of the 1956-57 season was just like any other season—I couldn't get off the ice, I played so much.

It all started because of the Players' Association. We announced the Association in February, 1957. After that, the teams in the league started to do some things.

Teddy got traded to Chicago over the summer. Never mind that in '57 in the whole league he was second to Gordie only in scoring. Never mind that he had 30 goals, and never mind that only three guys other than Gordie scored more

goals than Teddy did that season and one of them was The Rocket.

I mean, *come on*! Ted Lindsay was in his prime.

Jack Adams. I'm sure you've heard a lot of stories about that, what he's done to other players. Yeah, the teams in the league started to do some things.

Toronto lost a couple of guys that they got rid of the very same summer—1957—like their captain, Jim Thomson. Tod Sloan got sent to Chicago a year later. One of their best players and Leaf GM Conn Smythe didn't even bother to get a player in return. He sells his captain and his leading scorer to Chicago—for cash.

It was just stupid. When I think about it, they could have resolved it. It could have made our pension plan better, and the whole damn thing.

You know what? Some of these younger players today, I hope they appreciate some of the things that we fought for.

There's a lot of guys I played with who could really, really use a helping hand. I mean, they could really use it! The pension plan is so terrible that you can't get by on that. And, thank God, I'm in a situation, I don't depend on that pension plan. But, you know, not many of those guys are in that position.

The pension plan we have in hockey today, as far as the older players, is to me the worst pension plan going, compared to baseball and the other sports. You know that. You've heard that from other guys.

I remember when I came in the National Hockey League, Clarence Campbell—president of the National Hockey League at that time—used to come in and talk to us before every season. We only had six teams, so it was easy for him to do that.

So what happened was he comes in and we say, "Tell us about our pension plan," and so forth.

And he'd say, "You'll get paid back. All the money you put in, you'll get paid back."

So, I played 10 years in Detroit. I put all my money in the plan, all right? Now, I get $407.96 U.S.

And that's only because we won that lawsuit against the NHL a couple of years ago. Before that, I was getting about $300 in Canadian money.

I talk to some of those guys who play today, like we're talking now, and I say, "You guys should have gone back and fought for us."

The pension plan now, they've got a pretty good plan.

Stevie Yzerman was very, very interested. He wanted to hear all about it. Paul Coffey was the same way. They wanted to hear all about it: "Is it true?"

I told them the story. They wanted to hear. A lot of these young guys, they want to hear from the Original Six guys.

What happened was that we started our Players' Association in 1956-57. Teddy, he and I just kind of stuck along together.

There was only one guy in the National Hockey League who didn't sign up. And that was Teeder Kennedy, Toronto Maple Leafs. But Teeder Kennedy said, "But I won't squeal." And he never did. He never did.

Every other guy in the National Hockey League signed.

Rocket Richard, he was all in favor of it.

Everybody was all in favor of it.

Every club voted for it, except Detroit! Adams got Gordie and Red to topple on us.

Adams was doing things underneath the situation, trying to find out who the guys were behind the Association. And he found that out.

Then, of course, Jack would try to get guys like Gordie and Red to change their minds. Which, I think he did.

Gordie is a great hockey player, and so forth and so on, but I think Gordie didn't look at it the way that Teddy and I did. He just didn't. It's a free world.

Gordie held a lot of guys back because he could have demanded more money because he was the big gun.

It would be like the National Hockey League saying to Wayne Gretzky, "Well, we're not going to pay you."

It was the same thing with Gordie Howe at that time. He was the big guy.

All he had to say was, "Forget it. If you don't want to pay me, five other clubs will grab me; I'll guarantee you."

But Gordie trusted them. And that was a mistake.

Plus, I don't think Jack—I don't know this—but I don't think Jack was paid big money, either. He wasn't getting it, and we—Gordie or any of us—we were not going to get it.

We really didn't want anything more than we deserved. We just wanted to know more about our pension plan.

The owners wouldn't let us look in the books. They wouldn't let us do any of this stuff, and that's the reason why we actually started the Players' Association.

We said we didn't want unions. We said, "This is a Players' *Association*." If we'd have gone in as a Players' *Union*, that's a different story.

Then the federal government gets involved, and then you've got to expose all your books. Bruce

Norris was the owner of the Red Wings by then, and he was scared to death of that, big time! *Big time!*

We wanted to know what was going on! We found out when we went through this that they were supposed to match us dollar for dollar on the pension, all right? They were taking two-thirds of the All-Star Game revenue, and putting that in the pot, and then they were adding an extra 25 cents on the ticket in the playoffs, all right, but, you know what? That wasn't any money coming out of their pockets. It wasn't. The fans were doing it. OK? Then we found out that the owners were only putting in $600 to our $900.

But those days are gone. You can't look back.

Still, I was talking about how it's been, 55 years now since I broke into the National Hockey League—the other day, as a matter of fact.

My son and I were going over some clippings, and I said, "God, 50 years ago! It doesn't seem that way! I don't feel it."

I still think I'm young. I've always, as I said, been a positive thinker in life. I've always had goals in my life. I made myself reach. And, do you know what? It works. I've tried to teach that to my kids. And it worked for them, too.

Reminiscing sometimes, Teddy and I get together and talk and laugh, it seems like it's just been a few years ago, you know? That's right, just a few years ago.

JIMMY SKINNER

DETROIT RED WINGS HEAD COACH 1954-58

STANLEY CUP 1955

JACK ADAMS WAS MY SUCCESS. I really believe it.

Some of those managers today...I don't know. I just look and I wonder. I was lucky.

I was coach of the Red Wings in February, 1957, when Ted Lindsay tried to form a union on our—on all of us.

Ted Lindsay was a clubhouse lawyer. I'm going to say it! He was!

He tried to form a union.

Teddy was a hell of a hockey player. One of the best left wings I ever had. In fact, one of the best that I've ever seen in hockey, to tell you the truth. A good hard-nosed hockey player—put out 100 percent. He never bitched about being hurt or anything like that. He'd play being hurt. He wanted to play.

I can't criticize any of that. He was a dedicated hockey player.

His only trouble was his mouth. There are a lot of them like that.

He second-guessed me on the bench one night in New York. Carl Matson, our trainer, came to me after the period was over—it was a very important game—and we were leading, 2-1. He said, "That guy's second-guessing you on the bench."

I never benched him. I went in the room, I closed the door and I said, "Teddy, you know, I am fortunate to have a great left winger like you. You're one of the best left wingers in the National Hockey League."

The players all looked up.

OPPOSITE: Jimmy Skinner (Courtesy of Robert L. Wimmer)

"But until you retire and start coaching, mind your own damn business, and I'll coach the hockey club until then." And I walked out.

Players respected that. They figured I'd back down.

Jack Adams was good to Ted Lindsay! Once, Lindsay wasn't feeling good. He had a breathing problem. Jack came in the dressing room right in the middle of the season and says, "Here's a ticket. We want you to go to Florida. Stay down there until you get better."

They *never* tell those good stories.

They *never* tell about players that Jack helped.

Mud Bruneteau—when his father was very, very ill right in the middle of the season—he sent Mud home to be with his dad. Right in the middle of the season!

Joe Carveth, way back, when he and his wife had a family, they had baby girls who were blind. Jack called the team owner Jim Norris. They got the best doctors they could to try to help them out.

They *never* tell those two stories.

But, Ted Lindsay tried to form a union.

We took them down—Jack Adams, Mr. Norris, all of us—we took all the players down to the dressing room. We had the books out and everything. Let them look at the books!

We had, I think, six games left at home, and Jack or Mr. Norris, he says we're going to start making money now—the money that will carry us over for the summer. We were selling 12,000 tickets for every game at the Olympia, but we weren't making a lot of money.

Jack asked everybody all around the room, Red Kelly and all of them:

"Are you not satisfied with Detroit; the way you're being treated?"

Every Player: "Oh, we're very pleased. We're treated *wonderful*!"

So, Jack said, "Then what the hell's the matter with you? What do you want to have a union for?"

"Well, Toronto and Doug Harvey and Montreal Canadiens and Toronto Maple Leafs—they're not treating their players right."

We said, "What the hell's the matter with you? Worry about *them*? Worry about *yourselves*!"

That's *exactly* what happened. I was right there for everything!

Have you ever heard Red Kelly, Gordie Howe, Marty Pavelich or any of them criticize Jack Adams? I've never heard any of them.

I was really surprised when Jack Adams called me in Hamilton, Ontario, in the summer of 1954. I was just starting out; I'd just finished my first year as head coach of the Junior club Detroit sponsored, the Hamilton Cubs.

Adams says, "You're the new coach of the Red Wings."

But, Tommy Ivan was there in Detroit! He'd been there for seven years. Tommy had just won the Stanley Cup, again; his third as coach of the Red Wings.

I said, "Somebody's got to be kidding me. What happened?"

Jack said, "Well—Tommy—I gave him permission to go. Mr. Norris wants him to go to Chicago to help the Chicago club."

So, I was quite surprised about it. I was quite surprised. There was no job interview at all.

When we had some press releases, they had the number seven on them, because Detroit as looking for its seventh straight regular-season championship heading into the 1954-55 season.

I knew it was going to be a tough situation, winning that seventh in a row.

But, I was a rookie at that time. It didn't bother me that much. I didn't know how tough it was in the Stanley Cup playoffs and that. Junior hockey is a little different, amateur kids and that.

I was fortunate. When I coached Detroit, five or six of the players that I had in junior hockey—guys that I started off and developed— Glenn Hall, Terry Sawchuk, Dutch Reibel, Al

Arbour, Red Eye Hay—were up with the Red Wings. They knew me and they respected me from that.

I always treated them as my kids when I coached juniors. When you get those kids when they're 16 and 17, you've got to be a father to them. I *was* a father to them. I used to see that they got home.

So, I had a little gain on that. They knew me pretty well. They knew my way when I got mad; they knew how to take me. They knew my makeup and how I acted.

And I was fortunate enough to have an outstanding manager. You know, some coaches walk into a situation where they've never had a player before; where all the players are strange. Some coaches, they never had a good manager.

Jack was a good manager. Ninety percent of the coaching is your manager, I'm telling you. Jack Adams was one of those disciplined managers; tough-type managers. He was an *outstanding* manager; the same as Connie Smythe with Toronto Maple Leafs. That's discipline!

He backed me 100 percent during the year.

After a game, Jack would say, "Do you have somebody to drive your wife home? Come on up to the office."

We'd sit for an hour, two hours after the game. He always was good about it.

"Jimmy," he'd say, "This is constructive. Not

criticism. Why did you do this? Why did you do that?"

He remembered everything. He never made notes, but he remembered. He taught me from that.

I remember once, we gave up a goal and he wanted to know why Red Kelly wasn't on the ice.

I said, "Well, at that time Kelly had come off, he was really tired." I went to send him back out, but Kelly said, "Jimmy, give me a couple of more minutes."

But Jack didn't know that. He'd been asking me, "Why didn't you put Kelly back out?"

And I'd have to tell him what Red had said.

Jack used to send the odd message down to the bench, but I *appreciated* them. Because, to me, he was always constructive—it was always constructive information.

He'd send our trainer, Carl Matson, down. And Carl would say, "Jimmy, Jack says so-and-so isn't playing very well."

I was *fortunate* to get those notes from Jack! Maybe at the time, it used to bother me sometimes, but it used to bother the players more than it bothered me. Look, in football, they have spotters all over. Hockey's doing it now, spotters all over. Jack was just ahead of his time, that's all.

Other times, Jack, he got me on something I did wrong. But he'd straighten me out on it. You're never too big to learn from somebody else. I found that out a long time ago. My dad said, "Don't let your ass get on your chest." I've always remembered that.

To me, this is the best thing that ever happened to me. If I'd had a weak manager, *I* wouldn't have been any good.

I admire his loyalty. He always believed in loyalty. If he had players who played for him and were loyal, he always would try to look after them. He'd always try to get them jobs.

I never saw him cut a player's salary. Players used to come in and say, "Well, I think I deserve a raise."

He'd say, "Well, here's your record. You haven't improved *at all*, but I'm not going to give you a cut."

I remember a player came in there and said, "Well, Mr. Adams, I got married. I've got to have a raise."

"It's not my fault!" he says. "Look at your record. Play better, and you'll get a raise!"

Sure, he was a disciplinarian. That's what he was manager for!

Managers today are being fired because they haven't got discipline on their hockey clubs!

You see? *Discipline!* Discipline was the big thing.

I think it's the best thing! That's the trouble with kids today! No discipline.

The media keeps saying we got paid a piddling salary. It bothers me when they say that. I think they, the players, got paid. I worked for 56 cents an hour in the mines the summer before I turned pro! When Gordie Howe was getting $17,000, that was big pay!

The Detroit hockey club looked after their players very well. When we traveled on the road, Jack always had tickets for every stage show for them when they laid over in New York. He used to take them out and have steak dinners, stuff like that. It sounds piddling now, but we used to give them their meal money and all that; but then Jack would say, "Take them all out and have a little dinner for them." Or Mr. Norris, our owner, used to come in and we'd have a big dinner at some steak house, all the players. I don't think the other clubs did that. We, Detroit, treated our players very well. I can always say that.

I got started in hockey when I was a kid. A scout from Saskatoon scouted me when I was playing in the Saskatchewan Senior Hockey League for the Flin Flon Bombers.

I was just out of junior, and in 1944 he sent me down to training camp in Detroit. I played a few exhibition games. Lindsay was there.

I guess Jack took to me when we were working out at the Windsor Arena instead of over at the Olympia. It was very, very hot. Jack came in after practice one day and said, "We need a few extra players for our second shift. They practice at 6 o'clock."

Everybody was tired as the dickens—soaking wet—and he said, "We want some volunteers."

I knew *I* needed a little extra, so I volunteered. There were only about three or four of us volunteers who came out and skated with the guys who had to practice at night because they had war jobs.

I think, looking back, little things like that, you don't realize at the time, but they can really help you.

I was the last cut for the Detroit Red Wings at camp in 1944. Cully Simon was a holdout on defense. Adams said, "If Simon doesn't sign, you're staying up."

But, Cully Simon signed a couple of days before the league opened, so he sent me down to the American League, in Indianapolis. I never made it to the NHL; never played a game up there.

In 1945-46, they sent me to Detroit's farm team in Omaha, Nebraska, in the USHL. We played in Omaha together, Gordie Howe and me. It was Howe's first season pro down there. Gordie was a big gangly kid; 16 years old.

Gordie had so much power, and he was such a good hockey player that sometimes he'd give a little bit lackadaisical. A little chippy, you know? He'd get cheap penalties. He used to come from behind and trip a guy with his foot and stuff like that.

They had a hard time breaking him of that. Jack eventually got through to him. Gordie finally listened to Jack.

Gordie used to sit in the dressing room and get more bawling outs from Jack Adams than any of us! And Gordie took it. Favoritism is a bad thing in sports.

All the time I was in the minors Jack kept contacting me, asking me, "How are you doing?" Stuff like that. He took a liking to me. I never caused any trouble. I never drank. He was a non-alcoholic, and he liked that. I never bothered anybody. I kept my mouth shut. I never gave them any trouble.

When I started coaching the junior club sponsored by Detroit, the Windsor Spitfires, I used to phone him. I had players like Larry Hillman and Al Arbour. I'd say, "Jack, *you've got* to take these kids up in pro."

I was hurting myself. But I was dedicated to the Detroit hockey club. That's what my job was. And he admired that because he said a lot of coaches didn't want to give players up from their junior clubs until they were finished with their junior eligibility. Little things like that; that kind of sold him on me.

He always was honest with me. He said, "I'd *like* you to win the Canadian Junior championship—the Memorial Cup—but I don't give a damn if you do. I want those players trained that they know how to hold a hockey stick and how to shoot the puck. We get players who don't know the fundamentals. Metro Prystai come up,

and he doesn't know how to keep a puck on the ice! He puts it in the fans; in the stands all the time. Why don't you teach all of them a little fundamentals? We don't want Tommy Ivan to be wasting his time showing these pros all the fundamentals."

I listened to what he said. I spent a lot of time with the kids; all those players. Al Arbour was a forward when he came to me. I knew he couldn't score goals, so I made him into a defenseman. Red Eye Hay was a forward. Marcel Pronovost was a forward. I made defensemen out of them. I think little things like that impressed Jack.

So then, in 1953-54 I was sent over to Hamilton, and we had a pretty good year there with Detroit's Junior club. All of a sudden, I got that call from Jack saying, "You're the new coach."

He said, "You've got qualifications to be a coach." I never thought about that. I was happy where I was. I was surprised; I was really surprised.

My first Red Wings team, 1954-55, was an easy team to coach.

Start in goal. I wouldn't trade Terry Sawchuk for Patrick Roy any day. I'm not taking anything away from Roy, but Sawchuk was a dedicated guy.

He'd swear *at me* if he let a bad goal in. John Walter, the Detroit sportswriter, sat beside him in New York one night after we'd lost, 1-0.

The 1955 Cup presentation. (Courtesy of Robert L. Wimmer)

"Terry, now *how* did that goal go in?"

Terry says, "Bleep you." That's the way he was, you know? He was very surly.

We had two good goalkeepers, Terry Sawchuk and Glenn Hall. I had both of them in Junior hockey. We sat down, Jack and I, and Jack says, "We can't keep both of them."

Jack got criticized for trading Sawchuk. But, put yourself in a position like that. You can't keep a guy who's a National Hockey League goalkeeper

sitting on his fanny. So Jack says, "We've got to trade one of them."

Sawchuk was with us, and he was still young. We had to make a trade.

With that 1955 team, with all those stars, you knew you had the talent. But there was a lot more to it than that.

You know what burns me? In the Hockey Hall of Fame, they've got categories for everything, but they haven't got a category for checkers.

They've never recognized guys like Marty Pavelich, Metro Prystai—all those checkers.

When Marty Pavelich and them come off the ice, you could hear them:

"The S.O.B.s haven't scored against us!"

They weren't worried about scoring goals. They were worried about having anybody score goals *against us*.

Put *the checkers* in the Hall of Fame. They were as valuable to me as Gordie Howe, Ted Lindsay and those fellows!

You see former NHL coach Don Cherry on TV, former referee Red Story and all of those guys— knowledgeable hockey people—being asked, "Who was the best defenseman you ever saw?"

They always say, "Bobby Orr."

B.S.! Bobby Orr was a good *offensive* defenseman. Doug Harvey was the best *all-round* defenseman I ever saw. He could handle the puck in his own end, play the power play, kill penalties, control the game in his own end, control the game on the power play—*you name it*. Bobby Orr couldn't hold Doug Harvey's stick. Defenseman? He wasn't a *defenseman*. He always had a stay-at-home defenseman with him.

Why isn't Bobby Goldham in the Hall of Fame? The best stay-at-home defenseman I ever saw. I've seen a lot of them, way back, Black Jack Stewart, all of them. Bobby Goldham couldn't

carry a puck over the blue line, but I would take him ahead of any of those defensemen. I mentioned to one of the Hockey Hall of Fame judges that they never mention his name. Harry Howell, Ferny Flaman; they couldn't hold Bobby Goldham's hockey stick. It's a crime, it's a shame. I think the people who are voting on Hall of Fame now are younger people. They never saw them play.

Another guy they underrate is Alex Delvecchio. You never hear much about him. He never got the credit that he should have gotten. He's one of the best center-ice men *ever* in the National Hockey League. He could have been a superstar. He was a star, but he could have been a superstar. Alex was an easy-going guy, did his job, and was satisfied.

He was good for Gordie! Every player they ever put with Alex Delvecchio, that we got from trades or anything like that, all had good years. Alex was an outstanding center. He was the easiest type of hockey player to coach. Easygoing— never give you any trouble. Never! It was a pleasure to be on the same team with him.

They *all* tried to help me—Red Kelly, all of them. There wasn't *one* of those guys who said, "Oh, look. There's a rookie guy trying to replace Tommy Ivan. We'll take advantage of him."

It was quite the opposite, in fact. The players respected me. Respect is the big thing in coaching. To me, at least 60 percent of coaching is gaining the respect of the players.

Gordie Howe and Sid Abel. (Courtesy of Robert L. Wimmer)

That first year, Gordie came to me one night in Boston after we lost a game, 2-1. I was sitting on the trunks outside the dressing room. Gordie came down and sat beside me.

"Jimmy," he says, "I had a bad game. What am I doing wrong?" Gordie was a big star, but he was very, very, very modest.

I said, "You're not doing anything wrong. You just had an *ordinary* game." What are you going to say to a star like that who was excellent in hockey? But he respected me, so he came to me.

I'll tell you a story about Gordie:

We had practices *every day*. I said, "Jack, there's a lot of strain on the players. We play Thursday, Saturday, and Sunday. Let them have Monday off."

He said, "I'm not going to let them off on Monday. They have to come for practice, because if they don't, they stay at home; they lay in bed all day."

Gradually, though, I got Jack convinced to let us go down Grand River Avenue, a few blocks from Olympia, and have bowling every Monday morning instead of practice.

We did this a few times, and Gordie was never there. You know what? Howe was always back at the Olympia skating! He'd be out in the dark, skating around. We had to give him hell for being out there skating—with the lights turned off—instead of bowling with us.

I've been asked questions at banquets, "Who's the best hockey player between Howe and Maurice Richard? Who would you take?"

Richard was an outstanding hockey player, but not because I'm prejudiced or that, but I would have to take Howe.

I could put Howe on defense, I could put him at center ice, I could put him at right wing, I could have him kill penalties.

Richard was the better hockey player from the blue line in, as far as scoring goals, but that was his big thing. *Gordie Howe had everything.* That's why I would take Howe over Richard, any day.

If you put Howe, Wayne Gretzky and Mario Lemieux in front of me, I'll still take Howe, any day.

Mario Lemieux can't play defense. Wayne Gretzky can't play defense. They'd be knocked

on their asses every time they played hockey. Sure, they're great hockey players—in *this* era.

In the old era, Gordie Howe and all those guys played 14 times in the regular season against the same club, plus exhibition games, plus play-off games—every year. These guys today, maybe see a club twice a year.

Pronovost and those guys used to say things like, "Now, Jean Beliveau, watch when he comes down. He always goes to the left, 90 percent of the time." They studied it like a catcher in baseball studies the batters.

They shouldn't compare the two different eras! Six-team league's a lot tougher. And the players were tougher.

Of course, Gordie was tough. It sounds silly, but Gordie was mean, but Gordie was also a *clean* hockey player. As long as a player didn't bother him or do anything, he never bothered him. But if they started to bother him, he'd give it to them.

Bill Gadsby was a good, tough hockey player. When he hit, they knew they were hit. Black Jack Stewart was the same way. Red Kelly was a clean hockey player—too clean. Marty Pavelich was a clean hockey player—but he didn't take anything. Tony Leswick was a tough little guy. Red Eye Hay was a tough kid. Leo Reise was a big, tough defenseman. And they never mention those guys.

Now they're putting rules in—new interference rules. They are going to kill hockey. Howe and

Richard, and those guys, had guys hanging on to them. They'd give them an elbow! They'd look after themselves!

They've got hockey players out there now who say, "I've got to get out of the road. If I touch you, I'm going to get a penalty."

games left—one in Boston and back to back against the Canadiens—one at The Forum in Montreal and one in Detroit at the Olympia. The Canadiens were still leading us, though, and only had to get a tie out of the two games to clinch first place. We had to win them both or we would finish second.

> "I hardly watch it [hockey], because now they're getting all those cheap penalties. I'm so sick of it! Maybe I'm wrong, I don't know."
>
> —JIMMY SKINNER

I hardly watch it, because now they're getting all those cheap penalties. I'm so sick of it! Maybe I'm wrong, I don't know.

We had a lot of things happen in 1955, which gave a lot of incentive for the players. But the biggest thing was the tear gas in Montreal right before the playoffs.

Late in the season, just a month to go, and it looked like Montreal was going to finish first, and that we *wouldn't* get that seventh straight regular-season title.

Then, toward the end of February, we got hot—really hot. We won a game on February 20, one month to the day from the end of the regular season. We didn't lose again until the second round of the playoffs that year.

Heading into the last week of the season in mid-March, we'd won six in a row and had three

First, though, we had to beat Boston. We went to the Boston Garden—which was the first game there after Rocket Richard got into a fight with Hal Laycoe and wound up punching a linesman. That had happened on Sunday. We played at the Boston Garden on Wednesday.

While we were in Boston, we found out NHL president Clarence Campbell had suspended the Rocket for the rest of the regular season and the whole playoffs.

It was a close game that night at Boston Garden. Jack Adams was very sensitive, very nervous. He never could watch the full game. He'd go outside walking in the third period, but he could hear the yells.

When we came off after the game, Jack, because he's going by the noise from the crowd, comes into the room and says, "Well, we lost that one."

I said, "No! We won it, 5-4!" His face brightened up, just like that.

The next night, Thursday, March 17, we went into Montreal, where we had them, 4-1, at the end of the first period, with Richard being suspended.

We were in the dressing room after the first period, and I looked at my watch, and suddenly I said, "There's something wrong. We should be out on the ice."

We didn't know it just then, but the fans lost their cool and started the riot. The Montreal fans went out and attacked Mr. Campbell in the stands that night, and they had to get him out of the Montreal Forum. They threw the teargas, and we couldn't play because the gas was strong. We had put towels down on the bottom of our dressing room door to keep it from seeping in.

Mr. Campbell came in with the Montreal manager, Frank Selke, and said, "We're forfeiting the game."

Mr. Selke came in with a little piece of paper—it's in the Hockey Hall fame now. It was a note from Frank Selke, the manager of Canadiens, to Jack Adams; just written out that the Montreal Canadiens forfeit the game.

We were all surprised. And then Jack says, "It's time to get out. Go out the back way. We're going to catch the train out of Mount Royal. Don't argue with anybody. We might have a riot."

The French fans went down St. Catherine's Street and turned cars over, broke windows and that. It was quite a thing.

Three nights later, Sunday, we were home to Montreal on the last night of the regular season. We were tied with the Canadiens for first place. Anything but a win for Detroit and our streak of regular-season titles would be over at six.

No problem. We beat Montreal, 6-0, to finish the year with nine wins in a row, and we finished first by two points over the Canadiens.

It was Dick Irvin's 15th and last season as the coach in Montreal. He hated Detroit! Irvin couldn't help—nearly every day—criticizing the Detroit Red Wings: "All they do is throw the puck in. They're not a good hockey club."

I'd buy the Montreal paper and I'd just put it up on the board in the dressing room. I never used to say anything. I'd just put it up, and the players would casually go over and read it. We'd have our meeting, and you could see they'd been reading it. So, I never had to say much other than, "Well, we're playing Montreal tonight."

We had to talk more when we played Chicago or Boston, the bottom-place clubs, because we'd get lackadaisical against them. They always seemed to be saying, "Oh, we can just throw our sticks out there and we'll beat those clubs." Let me tell you something. We had a hell of a time beating Boston.

But, they *hated* Montreal and Toronto.

"Being hired by the Detroit Red Wings to be coach after they won the championship so many times. That was my biggest thrill!"

—JIMMY SKINNER

In Toronto, Lefty Wilson, our trainer, used to yell at Carl Voss, the referee-in-chief. Campbell called and said he wanted to have a meeting with us. Jack Adams went down with Lefty to Montreal for a special meeting for them. I was with them.

Campbell said that the NHL was thinking about suspending Lefty. Jack stood right up and said, "Mr. Campbell, *you* don't suspend any of my players. *I'll* do the suspending."

We swept Toronto in the first round of the 1955 playoffs, and only gave up six goals to Maple Leafs in the four games. Now we had won 13 games in a row.

We had home-ice advantage in the Final, and we pounded Montreal in the first two games in Detroit, 4-2 and 7-1. Now we had won 15 straight games—an all-time NHL record.

Then we went into Montreal, and the Canadiens tied the series, beating us, 4-2, in Game 3, and 5-3 in Game 4.

We came back home and handled them, 5-1, to take a three-games-to-two lead in the Final.

We went back to Montreal and lost Game 6 at the Forum, 6-3. So, it was back to Olympia for Game 7.

We stayed in Toledo at that time, and we came back in to play that Game 7 that night, and Marty Pavelich says to me, we were on the bus— I was quite worried—he said, "Jimmy, don't worry. We're going to win this hockey game."

He was right.

We came out onto the ice at the Olympia for Game 7, and I never heard a cheer like that in all my life—in all my time in hockey! I knew right then when I heard that cheer, we were going to win the game, which we did, 3-1. And there was no worry that night.

One of the sportswriters said to me after I won the Stanley Cup, "Is that the biggest thrill you've ever had, winning the Stanley Cup?"

"No," I said.

"Then what *was* your biggest thrill?"

"Being hired by the Detroit Red Wings to be coach after they won the championship so many times," I said. "That was my biggest thrill!"

9

GORDIE HOWE

DETROIT RED WINGS 1946-1971

HARTFORD WHALERS 1979-1980

STANLEY CUP 1950, 1952, 1954, 1955

HOCKEY HALL OF FAME 1972

YOU'RE A GOALIE, ARE YOU? How about that? I started in net myself. So, I know how that feels—to have that puck go in the net behind you. Oh, yes.

In Saskatoon, growing up, when I was trying anything I could to make the team because I was a younger guy playing with the older guys, I played goalie. And I could stop a few.

"Sudden Death" Hill, Mel Hill, remember him? He played for Boston. He scored three overtime goals in the 1939 playoffs. That's how he got that name, "Sudden Death." In fact, he was the only player ever to score more than one sudden-death goal in the same playoffs until Leo Reise did it for us, scoring two overtime goals for the Red Wings in the 1950 playoffs against Toronto.

Hill was from Saskatoon. One time he got hurt and he was back home working himself back into shape. So they put me in there and he's shooting on me. In those days I would say maybe four guys on a NHL team could shoot the thing around 90 miles an hour, which goes 60 feet before you can react. Hill was one of those guys. I'd make faces when I made the saves. Well, hell, the pads were only this thick! That son of a gun hurt!

They are shooting it harder today, but now the equipment is so big. The chest protectors are huge and then they started on the damn gloves. You know, they never even had a catching glove with Bill Durnan. He never caught the puck.

OPPOSITE: Gordie Howe. (Courtesy of the *Windor Star*)

He batted it down. Then he could use his stick better because he could use both hands.

So, the next day Hill came in to the dressing room and handed me the regular shin pads. When I dropped my pants to put them on he said, "Where's your jockstrap? Where's your cup!"

I said, "I don't have one."

He just rolled his eyes and said, "Oh, jeez!"

So, that was on guts alone that I made that team. That and because I was just a silly kid willing to try anything—including playing goal without the proper gear—to make a hockey team.

I didn't play goal for very long, though.

A few years later, the year before I signed with Detroit, in fact, I went to the New York Rangers' training camp in Winnipeg. They wanted me to go play junior in Saskatchewan at Notre Dame Cathedral. That's right; I'd have been a Hound. Maybe later I'd have been a New York Ranger.

But, I wasn't wild about the idea of going to Notre Dame. I wasn't a Catholic to start with, and my education process was not that good. I think I'm dyslexic—with the backwards vision. I think I had that. It's just a position where you're big, tall, and awkward. It took me a while to get coordinated. Even with my hockey. I had that kind of trouble, so when somebody from the Rangers asked me at a big function to get up and say a few words I said, "If I do, I'll never

be back here again." And they said, "No, you'll be all right."

"No, I won't." But, I said, "I won't let you down. I'll get up and talk as best I can, *but I will not be back.*"

And, because of them making me do that, I never did get back to the Rangers.

I'll tell you one thing that helped me a lot with that awkwardness. In Detroit, Terry Sawchuk and I spent a lot of time riding around together. Some of the guys on the club were doing crosswords. Terry was extremely good at it. I don't know why. Because goaltenders are smart? Yeah, he's got to use his brains somewhere. Ha, ha. So, I'd sit there and watch and he'd say, "You should know this one."

Pretty soon I got the pen and I started working 'em myself. The Detroit papers were good for me. I got to the point where I'd get about 90 percent of them. And I'd keep that one and the next day I'd get my answer. That was my self-education, really.

The year after I went to the Rangers' camp I came to Windsor for Detroit's camp and Jack Adams signed me and assigned me to the Galt Red Wings in the Ontario Hockey League.

Oh, my year in Galt! That was a whole year of sitting! I didn't play at all that year. I was learning.

Murray Armstrong, the coach, he called me up and he realized that he couldn't play me for the

Gordie Howe (#9) laces 'em up. (Courtesy of Robert L. Wimmer)

year because there was already three western boys on the team. They had a rule in the OHL then that each team could sign only three players from western Canada.

Armstrong talked to me and he said, "If you go home you'll do what, play for four teams and get in 20 games a year? What are you going to do? What are you going to learn? With your talent you're going to teach them. They are not going to be teaching you. It's going to be hard to do, but I will play you."

I was, I was really, really a little confused about that since I'd already been told I wouldn't be allowed to play in any league games.

Armstrong said, "You won't get off the ice in practice. You will play against the best there is in this league. And you'll practice power plays and you'll practice killing them. You'll play the different positions."

He said, "We'll get you where you want to be."

And he did.

But, when I think about it, it was Tommy Ivan, more so, more than Jack Adams even, who gave me the break I needed. When I played with Omaha Knights, the year after I'd been in Galt, my first season of professional hockey, Tommy was there. Tommy treated me very, very well. He'd have us over for Christmas. He did all the kind things.

I remember my first game in Omaha. I was very young. I was only 17. I'm playing and I got into

a little scuffle with a big, bald guy by the name of Harry Dick who played for the Kansas City Pla-Mors. He's a huge guy. I popped him about five times. While I was punching him, his right hand kept going back and back and back. When he finally released it I jumped in the air and he hit me and I went 15 feet back! And I started laughing. So when I look up at him he said, "You crazy blank-blank-blank."

Later on, wouldn't you know it, even playing against him, we became pretty good friends.

At first, for the first few months of the season in Omaha, Tommy never let me play. He had me sit at the end of the bench where the other players would have to partially crawl over me to get on the ice. He was teaching me by having me watch. He'd say, "Don't get down to the end. Get in there where you can bump shoulders with the boys coming in because if you go all the way down to the end, you're locked down there."

One night, I think it was in December, I got in a fight and I did okay for myself. So the next game Tommy put me in at right wing. I never missed a shift from that point on. It was that fight! That really impressed him. He thought that I had matured and I could take care of myself, I guess.

At the end of the season, Jack Adams called Tommy up to a meeting in Detroit.

Adams sat Tommy down and he threw papers on the desk with the names off all the players in the Detroit organization and said, "Tell me who's going to be with us. What do we need? Who's going to move' up from your club in Omaha to Indianapolis in the American League? I've got to know these things."

Tommy made a list of the guys he thought should be in Omaha and those he thought should be in Indianapolis and slid it back across the desk and said, "I'm all done, Jack."

Jack ran his finger down the list and threw it back at Tommy and said, "Finish it."

Tommy said, "It *is* finished."

"Well," Jack said, "Where's the Howe kid?"

Tommy said, "He's going to be with your club here in Detroit." He earmarked me, and boom, just like that, I was in Detroit.

When I left Omaha, Tommy smiled and told me, "Just keep doing what you're doing. And get to know the names of your new teammates!"

I had *great* teammates. So many guys helped me out; so many.

It was nice to have a guy like Sid Abel around. Sid was our leader. He came up and he told me one time, "What are you doing in the corners?"

I said, "That's my job."

And he says, "Well, when I'm in the corner, who am I going to pass it to?" He said, "You find your place where I can get it to you in front of the net somewhere."

Sid was the kind of guy who, at around Christmas time said, "Who doesn't have a place to go?" And, about three or four of us didn't, and we were his guests for the evening. In the summertime he didn't let the group get apart; the ones who stayed in town. They'd be in a bowling league. So, it was good. Detroit was really good. You can remember the early days when Sid was there and we'd start a situation on Monday nights, maybe once a month, where we'd meet and take over a whole restaurant. And that's where we'd have a dance or our Christmas party. We'd dance and have something to eat and that would be it.

And if you didn't show up and you didn't let anybody know you weren't going to be there you'd have to pay anyway. So, we were only making about $6,000 a year. You showed up! I don't care who it was.

I roomed with Ted Lindsay. He was my roommate. And we stayed by ourselves in one little home. Then we got an opportunity when Ma Shaw had Jack Stewart, Bill Quackenbush, Harry Lumley, and some of the older guys. So, when they gave up the game of hockey, then we moved in there for a while. And then Ted got married and I got married.

Jack Stewart was another one of the guys I watched and looked up to and learned from. To keep in shape in the summertime, Black Jack Stewart threw hay—bales of hay—bare-handed. So, as you can imagine, he was extremely powerful. So, that's what I did to try to build myself up. Not bales of hay, but I threw gravel. About eight hours a day pumping gravel in the off sea-

son. You see, sacrifice is never over when you are playing hockey. You can be leading the league in scoring and everything and if you relax a little everything goes by and you start getting hurt and you wonder why.

I measured Jack Stewart too, on the ways that he prepared for a game.

Ted Lindsay and I used to have to help him out of his berth when we took the train. He was in that bad a shape with his back and other things. We'd just about have to carry him off the train, and that night he'd still be out there punching and racking everything in sight!

I picked up a stick of his one day and it was like a big, heavy log. I said, "How do you shoot with this thing?"

Stewart said, "I don't. I break arms."

That was basically his mode, his frame of mind. It was. As I said, he was exceptionally strong. When you came down, he'd put his arm out. It was like hitting a telephone pole! It just hangs you. You don't go around it. If he got a few points, that was just an extra. All he did was sit in an area back on the blue line. Anybody tried to go through his territory; they were in a little bit of trouble.

Still, being on the same team, I never had anything to do other than watch him, except in practice when I played against him.

OPPOSITE: Ted Lindsay (left) and Gordie Howe. (Courtesy of the *Windsor Star*)

The strength of the individuals back then! One of the really strong, mobile individuals, in my book, was Tim Horton. He was just like Stewart. You'd go around him, he'd just grab his hand on you and you couldn't move. He was that strong.

There were quite a few feuds going on in those days, oh, yes. Black Jack Stewart had quite a few enemies. Big John Mariucci of the Blackhawks was one, for sure. As a matter of fact, one of the best fights I ever saw was Mariucci and Jack Stewart one night in Chicago. They were just milling around and Mariucci drilled Jack; drilled him a good one. And I jumped in. That's when Black Jack said, "You kids stay out of this!"

I was one of the kids, yeah. I was about 18 and he said, "You kids stay out of this! I'll fight my own fights, thank you very much."

It was funny.

It was an old western kind of fight, Stewart and Mariucci. Like, you hit me, bang! Ok, now it's your turn to take one. See who's going to be standing the last.

When I first came up to Detroit in 1946, I was worried about whether I could make it or not, yes. I felt that way for a while and then I ended up scoring 35 goals in 1950, my fourth season in the NHL. Then I wasn't worried anymore.

Of course, that's the year I got hurt in the playoffs. I got hurt in the first game of the first round against Toronto at the Olympia.

What happened? I have no idea up to a point. I came along and Kennedy had the puck and I was going to run him in the boards. I put my arm out and I took a look over to see either Sid Smith or whoever was playing the right side for Toronto so when I had my arms out in front of me like that I looked over and Sid was a little ahead of me, which meant my stick would be in the way so I leaned over. That was a mistake. When I leaned over, Kennedy's stick was there and bam! The stick hit me in the eye and then Jack Stewart hit me, too. And we all went into the boards.

I can remember a lot of what happened on the ice when I was laying there. I said, "I tried, I tried." That was my statement. That I was trying. Somebody, a doctor or a trainer—I don't know who—said, "We know you've been trying. You're okay."

Then I was out. I remember going to the hospital. Oh jeez, that ride on that stretcher! God, my head was just killing me. Then we went into the ambulance and got to the hospital and they wouldn't let me sleep. They kept prodding my feet and asking me questions, and then they got me up and looked at me and on the way back to bed I felt like I was going to be sick. The doctor said, "Get him back up here to the operating room," and that's when they did the operation. My getting sick, that's what made them operate on me. They drilled a small hole in my skull to relieve pressure on my brain.

The next day I woke up and I was not supposed to get out of the bed. Of course, I got out and went into the bathroom and I lifted up the bandage and I could see and I said, "Okay. I'm all right." My eyes were all right. That was a great peace of mind.

How, I have no idea, but I had this little toy water gun and somebody came in and said there was a surprise coming up. Somebody else had told me that Jack Adams had called my mother. When I got hurt, Jack Adams was the one who phoned home and he put my mother and my oldest sister on the plane and flew them down to Detroit, all the way from Saskatchewan.

When my mother came in, I looked up and whoosh—I drilled her with that water pistol.

So, she knew I was all right. It's harder on the parents, those things. But I was fine.

As for Jack Adams, sure I had respect. But it was tough. And let's put it this way, as far as the players were concerned, when Jack Adams wanted us, we were at his mercy.

At the time, he really took up a lot of our time as young people. Instead of having something fun to do, you'd be at a banquet. He'd come in and say, "I need four volunteers for the banquets on Monday and Friday."

And then he'd say, "The four will be Lindsay, Pavelich, Kelly and Howe!"

So we did it. We did it every time. It was so funny!

What Jack Adams did to me one time, he called me in and he said, "How good is your memory?"

"Not bad," I said.

Gordie Howe (#9). (Courtesy of Robert L. Wimmer)

"The last three days," Jack said, "Tell me what you've eaten; how much sleep you've got and what you've done."

My God.

So I said, "Well, I took a bus to the Olympia. After practice, I got dressed and then I walked home, about a four-mile walk. On the way, I stopped at the bowling alley and watched the bowlers."

And that, by the way, was a good stop for me. I'd met Colleen, my wife, at that bowling alley, so I made sure that was a walking day for me when I thought she might be there.

I continued, "There's a little shop I go in and they've gotten to know me and I'm friendly enough now so that I eat there every day, practically. Then, I went home, watched TV and did what I had to do. I did this and that, writing and answering fan mail."

I said, "I can't go by the minute but I would do that. And then I'd make sure that if there was a good show in town, I'd see it."

I told him what I'd been eating and he said, "Good, good."

Then I said, "Every now and then I go to the YMCA on the way home, and I go in and take a big steam bath and a little swim."

Jack almost came across the table: "Swimming! God, don't you know? There's air in your muscles before buoyancy. You're working to get rid of that air in the muscle! You need that air to build muscle in muscle! You stay out of that pool!"

And I said, "I didn't know. Thank you."

I left and then a few weeks later he had me back up in the office and he said, "Okay, now. Let's hear what you've been doing. Tell me just like you did before."

I said, "Ditto on everything, except swimming. I take the heat baths here."

He said, "That's very good, that's what we've got it there for. By the way, the last time I asked, your weight was what, about two-oh-six?"

I said yes.

"What is it now?"

I said, "202, or 203."

He said, "You keep that weight there. You never looked stronger."

So, after 32 years of playing, I was 204. I never strayed from that my entire career. Adams put that in my head. When we went out and I'd get little older and we'd have a beer, I wouldn't eat, if my weight was heavy.

Jack gave me the break. God, he's the one who ran the club.

Still, some of the things Jack Adams did were stupid. You'd win, but Jack Adams was always

Gordie Howe shows off the puck after scoring his 544th career goal. (Courtesy of Robert L. Wimmer)

thinking ahead. It was like a checker game. You make a move to make sure tomorrow is okay. And he didn't want the club to get too old.

We came to camp in the fall of 1955 the Stanley Cup champions. But Jack, he'd made so many moves over the summer that there were only nine of us left from the team that had won the Cup back in April, only four months earlier.

Terry Sawchuk was one of the guys he traded. How do you trade Terry Sawchuk? He led the NHL in wins in each of the five seasons he'd been with us. His goals-against never rose above 2.00 in any of those five seasons! *He won three Cups in those five seasons!* How do you trade a guy like that? *I* don't know.

But, with Glenn Hall ready to move up from junior, that was kind of an easy thing, I suppose. During Sawchuk's last year in Detroit, that 1954-55 season, Glenn Hall came up and took Terry's place and allowed two goals in two games, and so they knew he was ready for the NHL.

Sawchuk was a great goaltender. But he mouthed off. He said something.

The very same thing got Glenn Hall, too. Jack said something to him like, "We're all trying to help you," and Glenn said, "Well, what do you think I'm trying to do?"

You didn't talk back to Jack Adams. It was conversation that did them in, words. Conversation killed a lot of careers.

You didn't talk back *period* in those days. That's where hockey has changed now. Cripes, today you can say *anything*. And you can be quoted in the papers. If you did that when I played, you'd be gone. And I mean *you'd be gone the next day*!

Take Red Kelly. Red was hurt. He was playing when he was hurt late in the 1959 season. He was playing with a broken foot. They ran a story on it the following season with his quote, then they got rid of him.

It was total stupidity. Ridiculous. I just couldn't believe it.

Red was the best! He was very much a mobile defenseman like Doug Harvey. Red was a better skater. And he was strong.

The only difference between them was that Harvey would use his stick a little more on people. He used to go to his backhand so that when he backhanded the pass, the blade of his stick would come up and hit you in the face. He hit me once, and the next time I came back in there I kept one hand off the stick, and when he shot it I grabbed his stick and put it back in *his* face. I cut him with his own stick!

Lindsay was another one. Ted Lindsay did not care what Adams thought. He was feisty enough to say what he wanted to say. I was sitting at home with him one time and I said, "Why don't you just shut up? If you don't shut up, they'll move you!" That's the way I felt. And that's just what Jack Adams did. He traded Lindsay to Chicago. Like I said, conversation killed a lot of careers.

Gordie Howe. (Courtesy of Robert L. Wimmer)

Ted was my best friend, but we drifted apart. Why? Well, we never did anything the same. He didn't like golf. He didn't like fishing.

And some things happened between us.

I was really discouraged when we left Houston in 1977. We could have come back here. That would have brought things full cycle to play in Detroit with my two sons just like we had been for four years in the World Hockey Association in Houston after I'd retired from the Red Wings in 1971. The Houston club folded, and at the time I wanted to come home and spend a year with the kids playing in Detroit. The Red Wings weren't doing very well. In fact, they were terrible.

Ted was the general manager in Detroit by then. He said he didn't know if Mark could make it. He didn't know if Mark could make an NHL team? Holy cow! Mark was a left winger then, and then he went back on the blue line and became an all-star defenseman in the National League. He was another Red Kelly back there! People make mistakes, yes.

Then Lindsay said something about my wife, Colleen. I don't know why in the hell Colleen got to him but he said, "I wouldn't want her running into my office all year."

So that was that. Nobody picks on your family. Who the hell needs that?

But Lindsay always comes out and says some nice things about me now, so I can't say anything bad about him.

I was talking about how Lindsay always spoke his mind with Adams. I got mad at Jack Adams one time and spoke up.

Adams had taken a little run at Ted's wife, Pat Lindsay, and my wife, Colleen. It was 1955, I think. I'd gone into business with Lindsay and Marty Pavelich and Adams called the three of us, "The Business Tycoons."

So the wives showed up at a game at the Olympia wearing fur coats and handing out Monopoly money. They put their pictures in the paper wearing those fur coats. Fur coats, by the way, that they had borrowed.

Jack was livid and he said some things in the press that were not very nice.

So I said, "Can I say something to you, Mr. Adams?"

He said I could.

"You know, Mr. Adams," I said, "Colleen doesn't score goals. She doesn't assist. She's there at home, taking care of the kids and everything. When I play my game, she leaves the house in the afternoon so I can get my sleep. She's working 100 percent to help us this season, just as she does every season, and for you to call us 'business tycoons' and say things about the women is completely unfair and completely untrue."

And I said, "If you feel that way, I am not tied to this damn organization! Somebody else will want me if you don't!"

A banner honoring Gordie Howe adorns the rafters at Olympia Stadium. (Courtesy of Robert L. Wimmer)

I had never said a word to him before that. That was the first time.

You should have seen him back on his heels. His face turned bright red.

He started sputtering, "No, no, no! I didn't mean it. I'm just trying to show the young kids on the club nobody is above getting crap. This is a lesson *for them*. If we think you're not doing your job, we don't just pick on the kids; we pick on our established stars, too. The kids have got to know that!"

In those days, you just couldn't talk off the ice, but it was a little bit of a different story on the ice. We could talk to the officials, for example.

This kid from Boston gets me in the mouth with his stick one night so I have to get him back. I'm about to give him my stick when I hear Red Storey—he's the referee, yell, "Don't you do it! I'm watching you! I'll call it!" So I couldn't do anything. Not at that time I couldn't.

I got my turn, oh, like four or five shifts later and I drilled him. And he's down there and he's not hardly moving very well.

Red comes up alongside me and says, "You wonder why I didn't blow the whistle and call a penalty on you?"

I said, "It had occurred to me."

Red says, "Look at him. The bastard won't do *that* again."

We all tried to avoid misconduct penalties because they were so expensive—25 dollars. But most of the time the club paid it. If it was stupid on your behalf, you paid for it. But if it was in the course of trying to win a hockey game, the club paid it. I don't think I ever paid one. No, I don't think I did.

Not that I got that many. I got enough, though. Certain things you do, they don't like them. The only thing that really bothered me—in any game—if I got a penalty, a stupid penalty, and the other team scored and they went on to win,

to beat us, I'm letting down the guys I'm playing with. That bugged the hell out of me.

It bugs me that we didn't win more Stanley Cups. I played in the Finals 10 times and we won three of them. God, we could have won it more.

Take 1964. We're in overtime at home against Toronto leading the Finals three games to two. Bill Gadsby bounced it off the post and then they came right back down and got the winning goal. That was the night Bobby Baun of the Leafs came back with a sore foot after being carried off the ice on a stretcher in the third period. The bad thing was, Baun's shot hit Bill Gadsby and went in. Bill's never been on a Stanley Cup. He's a great hockey player that's never been there. That is a shame.

But the disappointments, they come and go.

You know, it's hard to believe it's all been so long ago now.

I just heard one of Marty's buddies, Marty's my oldest boy, got to be a doctor like Marty and he teaches medicine now. I said, "He teaches?" Then I thought, "Well, I guess he is about 49, now." So, yeah, the age bracket jumps up on you.

I look back at the times...it's hard to believe.

OPPOSITE: Howe closes in on the net.
(Courtesy of Robert L. Wimmer)